IS REALITY OPTIONAL?

IS
REALITY
OPTIONAL?

and other essays

Thomas Sowell

HOOVER INSTITUTION PRESS

Stanford University ◆ *Stanford, California*

With its eminent scholars and world-renowned library and archives, the Hoover Institution seeks to improve the human condition by advancing ideas that promote economic opportunity and prosperity, while securing and safeguarding peace for America and all mankind. The views expressed in its publications are entirely those of the authors and do not necessarily reflect the views of the staff, officers, or Board of Overseers of the Hoover Institution.

hoover.org

Hoover Institution Press Publication No. 418

Hoover Institution at Leland Stanford Junior University,
Stanford, California 94305-6003

First printing 1993
26 25 24 23 22 21 20   14 13 12 11 10 9 8

Library of Congress Cataloging-in-Publication Data
Sowell, Thomas 1930–
   Is reality optional? : and other essays / Thomas Sowell
      p.   cm. — (Hoover Institution Press publication : no. 418)
   Contains previously published essays.
   ISBN-13: 978-0-8179-9262-0 (pbk.: alk. paper)
   ISBN-10: 0-8179-9262-6 (pbk.: alk. paper)
   1. Social problems.   2. Social values.   3. Reality.
4. Civilization, modern-20th century.   I. Title.
II. Series: Hoover Institution publication; 418.
HM73.S686   1993
301.2—dc20   93-28078
                                        CIP

ISBN 978-0-8179-9262-0 (pbk)
ISBN 978-0-8179-9266-8 (epub)
ISBN 978-0-8179-9267-5 (mobi)
ISBN 978-0-8179-9268-2 (ePDF)

CONTENTS

◆ PART III: **THE ECONOMIC SCENE** ◆

◆ PART IV: **THE POLITICAL SCENE** ◆

◆   PART VIII: **RANDOM THOUGHTS**   ◆

INTRODUCTION

WHILE ESSAYS FOR NEWSPAPERS AND MAGAZINES tend to deal with one problem at a time, when they are brought together in a book, certain recurrent themes may become apparent. The essays that follow first appeared either in *Forbes* magazine or in my syndicated newspaper column (carried today by Creators Syndicate and in the past by the Scripps-Howard News Service), except for one essay reprinted from *The American Spectator* magazine ("Multicultural Madness"). Bringing these writings together now permits me to bring out some more general themes and approaches.

Amid all the wide-ranging political, economic, and social controversies of our times, some underlying patterns appear. On one side are those who see the problems of the world as being essentially subjective—not enough "compassion" or "commitment," for example—while those on the other side see reality itself as a severe constraint on what is possible, and the disregard of this reality as making many problems worse.

Those who see compassion, commitment, consciousness-raising, and the like, as the key to solving our problems are clearly in the ascendancy, which is why we hear such words so often. In their very subjective approach, intractable reality is often transformed into mere "perceptions." My first essay deals with this mindset by asking, "Is Reality Optional?" But the same question underlies many other issues discussed in the other essays: Are we free to believe whatever we choose or whatever is consistent with our prejudices, whether about Western civilization, the economy, or the credibility of Anita Hill? Is there no independent reality that we need to check these beliefs against? Are there no dangers in unfounded beliefs?

In many cases, the most elementary analysis of empirical facts is enough to destroy popular beliefs and devastate the assumptions behind those beliefs. The media or even academic intellectuals may choose to believe all sorts of things on all sorts of issues, but reality is not optional, as the essays that follow seek to demonstrate. These essays are reprinted virtually unchanged, except for correction of a few typographical or grammatical errors and an occasional clarification of wording that might have been ambiguous. But I have not allowed myself to become wiser after the fact than I was at the time. However, the titles may differ from the titles given the same essays by various newspaper editors around the country who published the syndicated columns, or by the editors of *Forbes* or *The American Spectator*. In the final section of this book, Part VIII, I have taken a number of columns in my "Random Thoughts" series and excerpted the best items from them to make one long column.

This book has been made possible by the conscientious work of my research assistant, Na Liu, who has tracked down hundreds of my newspaper columns and magazine essays, from which those reprinted here have been selected. They are reprinted with the kind permission of *Forbes* magazine, Creators Syndicate, the Scripps-Howard News Service, and *The American Spectator* magazine.

PART I
THE SOCIAL SCENE

IS REALITY OPTIONAL?

WHEN NINETEENTH-CENTURY WRITER AND LECTURER MARGARET FULLER proclaimed, "I accept the universe!" Carlyle's response was: "By God, she had better."

Now, a hundred years later, people who don't accept the universe are not only numerous but are also leading numerous political crusades.

The reality of limited resources and the painful trade-offs they imply are just so many lame excuses, as far as the environmental extremists or the Naderite safety fanatics are concerned. The very idea of taking economic constraints into account when human life is involved is scorned as morally unworthy. Yet a society's economic level is a major determinant of a people's longevity.

Big earthquakes in California do not kill as many people as smaller earthquakes do in Turkey or Iran, simply because the economic resources available in California permit buildings to be built to more earthquake-resistant standards.

If safety fanatics are allowed to kill the goose that lays the golden egg, that can also kill people. Already safety crusades are cracking down on the "pollution" of waterways involving traces of chemicals more minute than those found in tap water, sodas, beer, or even Perrier or Evian water. How much standard of living—which includes medical care—are we prepared to sacrifice in order to eliminate ever more remote dangers?

Even to ask such a question requires accepting the reality of economic constraints—and the trade-offs this implies. But those for whom indignation has become a way of life reject economics as readily as they reject history, geography, or anything else which implies that they cannot "have it all." Widespread use of the word "perceptions" is only one symptom of the notion that everything depends on how you choose to look at it.

It is almost as if the universe is optional.

Even the trade-off involved with a working mother has been waved aside with a phrase like "quality time," suggesting that the quantity of time lost between mother and child can be made up later by the quality. But when a child is frantic and sobbing at 10:30 Monday morning, that is when he needs his mother—and a trip to the zoo next Saturday is not going to make it up.

Those who promoted the banning of DDT and other pesticides, in order to eliminate the dangers created by residues, seldom take responsibility for the resurgence of malaria that followed.

If a trade-off has to be made, we can at least have the moral courage to face it, instead of kidding ourselves with words. Yet the intelligentsia go around saying things like "It's not a question of either/or," and using phrases like "win, win."

No part of reality is more intractable than geography, or more oblivious to our desires for equality. The peoples of the Himalayas have never had an equal opportunity to become great seafarers. The continent of Europe has virtually every conceivable geographical advantage over the continent of Africa, from navigable waterways to fertile soils to a more favorable climate and topography,

Yet neither geography nor economics nor even history are accepted as realities beyond our control. It might seem obvious that the past is an irrevocable reality, which our current wishes or perceptions cannot change. But that is not how many of our contemporaries look at it.

Any group whose past has not provided them with as many heroes, cultural contributions, or other glories as some other group's past now has a grievance against those who write history. Apparently a past to your liking has become an entitlement.

It is not even considered necessary to demonstrate any reality before claiming that a group's current "under-representation" in history books shows "exclusion" or "bias." Many of those who argue this way also loudly proclaim the many injustices suffered by the various under-represented groups. Yet, somehow, these pervasive injustices are not regarded as having inhibited the achievements of those who suffered them. Such is the self-contradictory vision of the multiculturalists.

In a universe without inherent constraints, there will obviously be "solutions" which depend only on our subjective "commitment," "compassion," and other feelings. Conversely, our failure to "solve" these "problems" shows only that most of us are just not as wise or as noble as the morally anointed who talk this way. There is absolutely no sense of the tragedy of the human condition among zealots.

Very few problems can or should be solved, in the sense of wiping out every vestige of them—not even crime or disease. Would anyone really spend half the Gross National Product to wipe out the last vestige of shop-lifting, or every minor skin rash?

The universe does not need our acceptance. Only our own well-being and survival depend on it.

---------------------- ◆ ----------------------

GRASSHOPPER AND ANT

JUST AS THE "ROCKY" AND "STAR WARS" MOVIES had their sequels, so should the old classic fables. Here is the sequel to a well-known fable.

Once upon a time, a grasshopper and an ant lived in a field. All summer long, the grasshopper romped and played, while the ant worked hard under the boiling sun to store up food for the winter.

When winter came, the grasshopper was hungry. One cold and rainy day, he went to ask the ant for some food.

"What are you, crazy?" the ant said. "I've been breaking my back all summer long while you ran around hopping and laughing at me for missing all the fun in life."

"Did I do that?" the grasshopper asked meekly.

"Yes! You said I was one of those old-fashioned clods who had missed the whole point of the modern self-realization philosophy."

"Gee, I'm sorry about that," the grasshopper said. "I didn't realize you were so sensitive. But surely you are not going to hold that against me at a time like this."

"Well, I don't hold a grudge—but I do have a long memory."

Just then another ant came along.

"Hi, Lefty," the first ant said.

"Hi, George."

"Lefty, do you know what this grasshopper wants me to do? He wants me to give him some of the food I worked for all summer, under the blazing sun."

"I would have thought you would already have volunteered to share with him, without being asked," Lefty said.

"What!!"

"When we have disparate shares in the bounty of nature, the least we can do is try to correct the inequity."

"Nature's bounty, my foot," George said. "I had to tote this stuff uphill and cross a stream on a log—all the while looking out for ant-eaters. Why couldn't this lazy bum gather his own food and store it?"

"Now, now, George," Lefty soothed. "Nobody uses the word 'bum' anymore. We say 'the homeless.'"

"I say 'bum.' Anyone who is too lazy to put a roof over his own head, who prefers to stand out in this cold rain to doing a little work—"

The grasshopper broke in: "I didn't know it was going to rain like this. The weather forecast said 'fair and warmer.'"

"Fair amd warmer?" George sniffed. "That's what the forecasters told Noah!"

Lefty looked pained. "I'm surprised at your callousness, George—your selfishness, your greed."

"Have you gone crazy, Lefty?"

"No. On the contrary, I have become educated."

"Sometimes that's worse, these days."

"Last summer, I followed a trail of cookie crumbs left by some students. It led to a classroom at Ivy University."

"You've been to college? No wonder you come back here with all these big words and dumb ideas."

"I disdain to answer that," Lefty said. "Anyway, it was Professor Murky's course on Social Justice. He explained how the world's benefits are unequally distributed."

"The world's benefits?" George repeated. "The world didn't carry this food uphill. The world didn't cross the water on a log. The world isn't going to be eaten by any ant-eater."

"That's the narrow way of looking at it," Lefty said.

"If you're so generous, why don't you feed this grasshopper?"

"I will," Lefty replied. Then, turning to the grasshopper, he said: "Follow me. I will take you to the government's shelter, where there will be food and a dry place to sleep."

George gasped. "You're working for the government now?"

"I'm in *public service*," Lefty said loftily. "I want to 'make a difference' in this world."

"You really have been to college," George said. "But if you're such a friend of the grasshopper, why don't you teach him how to work during the summer and save something for the winter?"

"We have no right to change his lifestyle and try to make him like us. That would be cultural imperialism."

George was too stunned to answer.

Lefty not only won the argument, he continued to expand his program of shelters for grasshoppers. As word spread, grasshoppers came from miles around. Eventually, some of the younger ants decided to adopt the grasshopper lifestyle.

As the older generation of ants passed from the scene, more and more ants joined the grasshoppers, romping and playing in the fields. Finally, all the ants and all the grasshoppers spent all their time enjoying the carefree lifestyle and lived happily ever after—all summer long. Then the winter came.

♦

FAMILIES UNDER SIEGE

THE FAMILY IS UNDER SIEGE TODAY as perhaps never before in history. It is under attack statistically as well as politically.

Clever sophisticates are forever citing statistics suggesting that the traditional nuclear family is already an anachronism. Only 26 percent of households consist of two-parent families and their children, they say.

Superficial plausibility is usually sufficient for political purposes, but what happens if we scrutinize that "26 percent" statistic more closely?

First of all, it excludes even the most traditional two-parent families *after their children have grown up.* Ozzie and Harriet would not be counted in these statistics, after Ricky and David grew up and left home. In fact, if the entire country consisted of nothing but Ozzie-and-Harriet families, the clever sophisticates could still say that only 33 percent of households were traditional, after Ricky and David began living elsewhere, in their own households.

George Bush and Barbara are not counted as a "traditional family" in the official Census statistics, even though they have been married for 45 years and have raised children, because those children are no longer living with them. Newlyweds are likewise not counted as a "traditional family," until they begin having children.

The family is also under attack in our public schools. Parental authority is undermined in innumerable ways, in textbooks aimed at children as early as preschool. If that seems incredible, read *T A for Tots* by Alvyn M. Freed (for kindergarteners to third-graders) or *Changing Bodies, Changing Lives* by Ruth Bell, et al (for high-schoolers).

The theme of all sorts of so-called "decision-making," "drug-prevention," or "sex-education" programs in the public schools is that the individual child must make his or her own decisions—and must do so independently of the values taught by parents. The very concepts of right and wrong are dismissed at the outset as mere prejudices of parents or "society."

The steady drumbeat of anti-parent themes continues right on through college. Cornell University President John Rhodes urged parents to "stand back, don't push" when time comes to choose a college. "Stop meddling" was the more blunt advice of an administrator at William & Mary College. An orientation session at Stanford, for parents of entering freshmen, has been full of advice for them to butt out.

The ostensible reason for all these efforts to get parents out of the picture, or at least moved to its periphery, is to allow the free development of their offspring. But the people most active in promoting this philosophy are very often the same people most active in promoting all sorts of brainwashing programs to impose a new conformity, under such misleading names as "diversity."

Perhaps most dangerous of all, the family is under seige from government. For example, the number of things a child can do behind the parents' back with the aid of government is increasing.

Most have to do with sex and its consequences. Abortion is the only operation that can be performed on a child without parental permission. The distribution of condoms, with the dangerous illusion of security they provide, has likewise become another direct government-to-child operation, with parents cut out of the decision.

The whole child-abuse industry, and the reckless propaganda surrounding it, is another government operation that not only reaches right into the heart of the family on flimsy pretexts, but also expands to include things that no reasonable person would consider abuse. Meanwhile, genuine child abuse is often lost track of in the avalanche of false reports inundating the system under bureaucratic rules and strident propaganda.

Why all these attempts, from so many quarters, to undermine the family, exaggerate its faults, and minimize statistically its very existence?

Many of the vital functions which families provide are functions which many wish to see provided by the state. Many of the traditional values which families pass on to the next generation are values rejected by clever sophisticates, who think that their superior wisdom should be replacing that of ordinary people.

Above all, families are the biggest single obstacle to the visions of the anointed, who take upon themselves the task of reconstructing society. Families care for their own, not for some abstract principle of imposed "equality."

The opposition of the political left to the family goes far back in history. The first draft of *The Communist Manifesto* made the destruction of the family an explicit part of its agenda. However, Marx was savvy enough to remove this excess candor by Engels.

Families are one of those independent centers of power which are intolerable to those who want to impose their ideologial Utopias from the top down. It is logically a prime target for unremitting erosion and undermining by those who dare not attack it openly.

————————————————————— ◆ —————————————————————

SAVING THE WHALES

A DREADFUL MEMORY FROM MY CHILDHOOD was seeing a chicken's head cut off, and watching the headless body run frantically around the yard until it finally collapsed in a spasm of death. Yet, somehow, all this was completely forgotten when the same headless body emerged later on the dinner table, magically transformed into appetizing pieces of Southern fried chicken.

Today, most people are insulated from the horror of the slaughter, and see chickens for the first time as neatly packaged sets of parts in a supermarket. The chickens, however, are no more insulated from reality now than they were half a century ago. Nor are the cows who become our cheeseburgers or the fish who are virtually unrecognizable in our tuna salad sandwiches.

Affluence buys insulation from unpleasant realities, as it buys many other amenities. Affluent societies and affluent classes are therefore likely to contain many very unrealistic people.

Insulation from the grim reality that life lives on the death of other life shows itself in outbursts of horror and indignation when deep thinkers suddenly discover the killing of some particular species that they find appealing. Their anger may be directed at their fellow human beings—especially whalers and other hunters—but the basic source of their outrage is that the universe was not built to their moral specifications.

In these times, it is often a short step from moral preening to political activism, or even direct interference with the livelihoods of other people. The media find it inspiring when insulated and affluent young people organize themselves to go interfere with those who do the dirty work on which all of us depend. This will surely go down in history as the golden age of self-righteous arrogance.

If someone wanted to argue that we should all become vegetarians, that at least could be debated. But to carry on about the killing of whales while eating cheeseburgers is a little much.

Of course, whales have feelings. So do chickens, lambs, and tuna fish. Even the lowliest creatures struggle frantically to hold onto life. If we refuse to kill whales, we are going to have to kill an awful lot of sardines to make up the difference.

The anointed don't like to talk about painful trade-offs. They like to talk about happy "solutions" that get rid of the whole problem—at least in their imagination.

One solution is to say that whatever they don't like—whaling, nuclear power, DDT, mental testing, etc.—isn't really "necessary." Before taking this kind of argument seriously, we have to realize that there is not a single food on this planet that is "necessary." But that doesn't mean that food is unnecessary.

Similarly, nuclear power plants are not "necessary"—if you are willing to build great numbers of new hydroelectric dams or use vast quantities of petroleum to generate electricity. But many of those who oppose nuclear power plants also oppose building dams or drilling for oil. Each, of course, is "not necessary"—but only when you have one of the others as an alternative.

There is no point trying to appease the anointed by giving in on some particular issue they raise, because that only shifts the fight to some other issue. The basic underlying problem is that they do not live in the grubby world of trade-offs with the rest of us. They live in the loftier realms of their own minds where "solutions" prevail.

Oliver Wendell Holmes once referred to people "criticising the order of the universe as if they were little gods outside it." The anointed may rail at the rest of us, but their real problem is that the universe was not built to their specifications—and shows no sign of bowing to their superior wisdom.

APOLOGIZING FOR CIVILIZATION

WHY DO PEOPLE CONTRIBUTE MONEY to the degeneration of the very society in which they live, and in which their children will grow up?

It happens every day, on the streets of cities and towns all across the country—in New York subways, in San Francisco parks, and in thousands of other places where begging on the streets has become a full-time occupation. Even in shopping centers with "help wanted" signs in the windows of stores and fast-food restaurants, people carry signs saying, "Will work for food"— not so that they will get either work or food, but so that they will be given hard cash.

All this is happening in a society with massive welfare-state programs covering virtually every conceivable problem—or claim of a problem. Begging provides supplementary income, sustaining drug and alcohol consumption, among other things.

Can anyone seriously believe that maintaining an army of idle people on the streets makes for a better society? Or that subsidizing irresponsible behavior is the way to get responsible behavior—either by the people involved or by those who see them getting away with it?

Would so many young people be able to devote so much time to gang activities if they had to make a living? Not all of them are living by selling drugs. Many are able to indulge their "lifestyle" courtesy of the taxpayers.

Even more remarkable than the growth in numbers—and in boldness— of parasites is the growth of a sickly sense of guilt toward them by people who pause on their way to work to give money to those who refuse to work.

Perhaps there is some sense of, "There but for the grace of God go I." Even in a secular age, that statement has a ring to it.

It is certainly true that you could have turned out to be a very different person if you had been raised a different way—or not raised at all, but allowed to grow wild, like a weed. But that is very different from the propaganda line that the homeless or other parasites are "just like everyone else."

The plain truth is that drugs, alcohol, or an irresponsible, hustling, or criminal mentality have flooded our streets with parasites. Mental illness has put some of the more heart-breaking cases on the street, instead of in custody. Perhaps a third of those wandering the streets are prey to the delusions of their own minds—and to the truly vicious among their fellow "homeless."

How did such a mess suddenly develop, in cities around the country, within the past several years? Indeed, it is a phenomenon also found in the streets of London and Paris—able-bodied people, often young and speaking in educated accents, shamelessly asking others for the money they are unwilling to earn to support themselves.

The most obvious reason is that they can get away with it. There was a time when the police would have put you in jail for pestering decent people as they went to work or headed home, or went shopping with their own hard-earned money. Then the courts and the American Snivel Liberties Union came to the rescue of the parasites.

To the morally anointed, all social outcasts are "victims" to be rescued, even if they were cast out for their own rotten behavior. Adopting wrongos as mascots puts a special shine on the halo of the anointed, and demonstrates their moral superiority to the rest of us.

By the same token, the anointed regard the ordinary, decent, law-abiding, tax-paying citizen as expendable. John Q. Public can be hustled on the streets while trying to get to work, or in an airport while trying to catch a plane. His children can be driven out of the parks that his taxes built by the sleazy characters who infest parks today, doing all sorts of shameless things in broad daylight.

Ultimately, however, we cannot blame it all on others. We elect the politicians who spend our tax money on parasites and who appoint mushy judges who create "constitutional rights" out of thin air to make it impossible for a society to defend itself against infestations of parasites.

We must also take responsibility for listening gullibly to all sorts of "advocates" for homelessness and other causes, as they regale us with statistics that they have generated to serve their own purposes. The media act as megaphones for all these unexamined numbers and unsubstantiated claims, but ultimately we are responsible for believing self-serving propaganda from zealots.

Most directly of all, it is we who reach into our pockets and pull out money to contribute to keep this social cancer going.

Worst of all, guilt has so furtively stolen into many hearts and minds that people feel apologetic about being civilized, educated, and productive when others are barbaric, uneducated, and parasitic. When civilization apologizes to barbarism, something has gone very wrong at a very fundamental level.

◆

BEING "WITH IT"

SHE IS THE VERY MODEL OF A MODERN MOTHER. When she had her baby, it was a family event in the delivery room. Not only was her husband present, but also other family members, including her 4-year-old son.

Photographs were taken during the delivery. These have been collected into an album that can be shown to visitors.

Now that the baby girl is home, her 4-year-old brother holds her. When he thinks nobody is looking, he sometimes drops her. This story is particularly horrifying because just a few months ago in New York, twin-baby boys died after their 4-year-old sister dropped them—also deliberately.

What can be the matter with parents irresponsible enough to leave newborn babies in the hands of 4-year olds?

It is more than just an isolated lapse in judgment. It is part of a whole new way of life in which being "with it" is the guiding light. Why so many people are so anxious to be "with it" at all costs is one of the great mysteries of our time.

Part of the reason is moral intimidation by "experts." Recently, a psychologist on the radio advised parents what to do if one of their children tells them, "Go to hell!" The way to handle it, the psychologist said, is to out-cool the kid. Don't let him see that it makes you angry.

Back in the old days, any kid who said that to his parents would not only have seen that it made them angry, he would have felt it—perhaps from a slap across the face that rattled his molars. But this modern psychologist's advice was given in lofty tones of total certainty. Hearing it, you would never dream that we had already messed up a whole generation of children by listening to "experts" like this.

Deep thinkers don't have to produce evidence that what they say works. All they have to produce is anxiety in the rest of us to be "with it."

Deep thinkers who advise students at Stanford University have said that it's OK for a woman to undress, get into bed with a man, and then decide to say "no." Now, that's being "with it"—not intelligent, but "with it." (Stanford women students average more than 100 "unwanted pregnancies" annually.)

Some of the trendy notions of our time are said to be "scientific" or "proved" by "studies." Many of the people who talk this way haven't a clue about science and have never seen the studies that are supposed to prove so much. Some of these studies are so crude and shallow that you wouldn't choose between Corn Flakes and Rice Krispies on the basis of such shaky evidence.

There is a well-established pattern to the way fad thinking takes over.

First, you are morally intimidated into believing that only the most ignorant, stupid, or hopelessly old-fashioned people resist the new wisdom, whose benefits are obvious, numerous, and great.

Then, when it turns out that the bright new idea makes things worse, you are morally intimidated by being called "simplistic" when you point out how the great promise has ended in disaster.

There are always "many factors" involved—and the burden of proof is then put on you by those who were so positive before, with no proof.

Remember how freer, less structured schools with fewer rules were supposed to lead to higher performance—and led instead to lower performance?

Remember how sex education was supposed to lead to less venereal disease, fewer pregnancies, and therefore less need for abortion—and how all three have skyrocketed at the same time?

Remember how modern theories of criminology were supposed to reduce crime—and how crime rates soared after these brilliant ideas became part of our legal system?

Remember how foreign aid was supposed to help poor countries feed themselves, get out of debt, and become friendly to the United States—and how the opposite of all these things happened?

All this was just part of the price tag for being "with it." Those who are "with it" are often wrong but never in doubt. Whether the issue is the environment, crime, or the survival of Western civilization, their top priority is asserting their own superiority.

Some things must be done on faith, but the most dangerous kind of faith is that which masquerades as "science." As the pretense of science has replaced commonsense experience, we have abandoned many old-fashioned practices that worked in favor of high-sounding innovations that have led to disaster.

If someone ever discovers why lemmings stampede headlong into the sea and drown, it may provide a clue as to why human beings are so anxious to be "with it."

◆

WISE MAN

"GREAT WISE MAN OF THE MOUNTAINS, I have travelled many miles and climbed many hills to reach your isolated hideaway. Will you answer some questions for me from your vast store of wisdom?"

"Yes. I have but one rule: You can ask only one question on a given subject."

"Thank you, great sage. You are most generous and—"

"Proceed."

"Can you tell me the secret of life?"

"Yes."

"What is it?"

"You have already asked your question on that subject."

"Oh."

"What is your next question?"

"What is so rare as a day in June?"

"A white basketball star."

"A riddle for which I have never been able to find an answer is this: 'What has lots of motion without actually going anywhere?'"

"I have two answers for you—a rocking chair and the Bush administration."

"Another riddle: 'What has eighteen legs and catches flies?'"

"I don't know the exact name but there is one crawling on your shoulder."

"Ugh! I thought the answer was a baseball team."

"It doesn't look like a baseball team to me."

"O wise man, when I was young, I was happy and gay——"

"Your sexual preferences are your own business."

"What I mean is, I was jolly and optimistic. I made friends easily. Now, 20 years later, I find myself more pessimistic and even suspicious of people. What caused that change?"

"Twenty years of experience."

"Wise man, what is the least intelligent form of life?"

"A committee."

"Can oil and water mix?"

"No."

"Can politics and honesty go together?"

"You have already asked that question."

"Man of wisdom, please tell me what to do. I am in love with a beautiful woman, but when I finally found the courage to tell her how lovely she is, she only replied: 'Flattery will get you nowhere.'"

"She could not have been more mistaken. Continue the flattery and take your vitamins."

"Great sage, would you buy a used car from House Speaker Jim Wright?"

"No—nor a new car either."

"Incidentally, I am a businessman who owns an automobile junkyard. Can you give me a name for my business that will sound fancy, so that it will impress upscale people?"

"Oedipus Wrecks."

"Wise man, who were the original odd couple?"

"King Kong and Faye Wray."

"What do you call people who can love something that aggravates them?"

"Parents."

"Who is more phoney, the politicans or the media?"

"That is too close to call, even for me."

"Are you really the wisest man in the world?"

"Yes."

"How did you manage to become so wise?"

"Sheer genius is my only secret."

"Why do you live in isolation and poverty?"
"I put my life savings in a Savings & Loan."

◆

THE GREEN BIGOTS
TURN BLOODY

GEORGE ANDERSON'S FACE WILL HAVE TO BE "RECONSTRUCTED," as the
doctors say. It was torn up by a sabotage device placed in a tree. Anderson
is a 23-year-old sawmill worker in California. When the saw hit the booby
trap imbedded in some wood that was being cut at the sawmill, Anderson's
face was ripped up and he also lost some teeth.

He could have been killed.

Why would anybody do such a thing? Very simple. Environmentalism
and the moral arrogance that goes with it.

One of the environmental extremist organizations publishes a book telling you how to put such booby trap devices in trees. When this particular
band of environmental zealots don't want you to cut down trees, they feel
that they have a right to stop you—or to take their revenge on you.

Apparently it is okay to destroy flesh and blood in order to protect wood.

The real mark of a bigot is that he claims rights for himself that he denies
to other people. By this standard, the environmentalist movement richly
deserves the title, "the green bigots."

Not all environmentalists condone bloodshed. But the whole movement
is based on the notion that what they want should be imposed on other
people. Once you go down that road, do not be surprised to find bloodshed
at the end of it.

Land, trees, waterways and other natural resources each have a thousand
uses—and many people who prefer and benefit from each of these uses.
There are many ways all these various people can share these resources,
including buying portions of each in open competition.

The green bigots want none of that. When they say "save" this or "protect"
that, they mean that the government should step in and forbid anybody from
using it for anything the environmentalists don't like. This is the spoiled

brat's vision of the world, where other considerations and other people don't matter.

Environmental restrictions on land have driven housing prices up astronomically in California—far beyond the ability of most working people to buy a home. Environmentalists have opposed the modernization of dangerous highways, even though people are killed on them every year.

Legally protected wetlands breed mosquitoes and other pests, and the diseases they carry. Protected "endangered species" of wild predators attack not only livestock but also children. Environmental restrictions on pesticides have permitted a resurgence of fatal diseases, especially in poor countries.

Although the government's environmental restrictions cost billions of dollars in lost jobs, housing, energy, and other uses, when the environmentalists do not get everything they want legally, many of them do not hesitate to get it illegally. Illegal obstruction and harassment of loggers, fishermen, nuclear power plant workers, or anyone else doing anything the green bigots don't like has become standard procedure.

Judges often give them wrist-slap sentences when they are caught—or no sentences at all. Both the law and the media treat them as nice, sincere people who want to do good things. This only feeds their moral egos and the intolerance that goes with it.

Sometimes the environmentalists have a point. The problem is that they don't recognize that anybody else has a point, much less rights. A steady diet of environmentalist propaganda is found on every nature program on television—and usually not one word of contrary opinion, fact, or analysis.

Despite many federal crackdowns on broadcasters who violate the "fairness doctrine," this longest-running propaganda bonanza on the air goes unchallenged. Even the book providing instruction on how to booby-trap trees has been publicized and defended on public television.

The idea that zealots who wrap themselves in a moral banner are somehow exempt from the rules has been growing—like a cancer. The green bigots have now turned bloody. It was only a matter of time.

It is only a matter of time before other zealots for other causes do the same.

◆

SCIENCE VERSUS UNISEX

STOP THE PRESSES! Science has discovered that women are different from men.

This shocking information came out of a meeting of the New York Academy of Sciences last month. Researchers reported that parts of a woman's brain are larger than the corresponding parts of a man's brain. "This anatomical difference is probably just the tip of the iceberg," said one neuropsychologist—a woman.

While most of us are probably not going to be unduly upset by all this, it will be hard to take for the anointed true believers, who are trying to build a unisex world. All differences between the sexes are due to "society," according to the dogmas of the anointed.

The "liberated" unisex types are unmoved by the fact that some kinds of disorders—autism, for example—are far rarer among girls than among boys. They say the magic word "society" and that explains everything. Nor have they been willing to budge when studies of unborn babies show different patterns between girls and boys.

The report on brain differences between the sexes is remarkable simply because it was reported. "Research on sex differences in the brain has been a controversial topic, almost taboo," according to the *New York Times* reporter who wrote the story. In other words, radical "liberated" feminists have intimidated people from saying anything that goes against their unisex dogmas.

The big bugaboo of course is that any discussion of any innate differences will lead to claims of female inferiority and be used to justify discrimination against women. But if there is any context in which sweeping labels like "superior," "inferior" or even "equal" make no sense, it is when comparing men and women. Both are indispensable to the survival of the human race, so one cannot be more indispensable than the other.

Numbers can be greater, less, or equal to one another because they have only one dimension. Men and women are simply different because they have many dimensions. How many of the male-female differences are due to nature and how much to social evolution, we do not know and may never know.

Radical "liberated" feminists are just one of many self-righteous groups who imagine that all the world's troubles are due to other people not being as moral or as wise as themselves. But many statistical differences between men and women have very straightforward explanations—if one is looking for explanations, rather than for another reason to feel morally one-up on others.

When a woman who has been out of the labor force for 10 or 20 years, raising a family, re-enters the job market, she does not have the same job experience or seniority as a man who has been there all the time. They are of course paid differently.

Much of the male-female income difference originates in situations where a woman's role as mother or home-maker limits her chances of maximizing her income in the job market. Nobody has sat down and decided that women are "worth" only 59 percent of what men are worth. Women who never married, and who worked continuously, have long held their own in competition with men in the marketplace—well before any "liberation" movements came along.

The paranoid feminist "liberation" vision tries to analogize women to racial or ethnic minorities. But a big part of the problem in racial and ethnic conflicts is that one group often knows little about the other and can easily believe the worst. Women and men do not grow up in different communities. The bonds between mother and son, father and daughter, brothers and sisters, or between lovers, are among the most powerful there are.

The bonds between men as a general group cannot begin to compare with these kinds of bonds. The paranoid vision that men as a general group conspire to subjugate women ignores the fact that no man wants to see his mother or his daughter discriminated against.

Mistakes have been made in laws and practices that distinguish men and women, as mistakes have been made in everything else that human beings have done. Some practices that may have made some sense in one era have continued through inertia and have outlived their usefulness. When that happens, reforms are in order—but not paranoia.

Unfortunately, many "movements" and "leaders" find paranoia useful for their purposes. But society is seldom benefitted by turning people against each other—certainly not women and men.

ABUSING CHILDREN—
AND THE TRUTH

EVEN SMALL CHILDREN who are toilet-trained sometimes have embarassing accidents. When this happened in nursery schools, it was once common for one of the adults to take the child to the bathroom, clean him up, and try to soothe his feelings.

Some nursery schools no longer do this. Today, such an act of kindness could lead to charges of sexual molestation. This is only one of the costs of the hair-trigger legal and political environment surrounding child abuse.

Currently the 9th Circuit Court of Appeals is reviewing the case of parents who were jailed for child abuse, on the unsubstantiated charges of a woman who had been fired by several nursery schools for her obsession with child molestation.

Tragically, this heedless and frenzied atmosphere is an international phenomenon, deliberately promoted. A series of scary magazine ads on the sexual abuse of children ran in New Zealand publications a few years ago, and were used to raise money, as well as to expand the activities of social agencies claiming to be able to deal with the problem.

Radical feminist activists were prominent among those promoting this campaign and proclaiming male oppression and the inadequacies of the traditional family. Statistics put out by those with a clear vested interest in hysteria and denigration of the family were as uncritically accepted in New Zealand as they are in the United States.

Fortunately, in New Zealand, a journalist named Emily Flynn decided to write a story about child abuse. Initially sympathetic to the claims that were being made, Ms. Flynn discovered that the sources and methods used to generate scary numbers were sloppy at best and dishonest at worst.

One ad featured a picture of a little girl in her bed holding a teddy bear, while in the background a backlit figure of a man stood in an open doorway. Above the picture, the headline proclaimed: "It's not the dark she's afraid of."

The caption under the picture asserted: "One in four New Zealand girls are sexually abused before they turn 18. Half of them by their own father."

Ms. Flynn could find no study to substantiate that claim, whether in New Zealand, Britain, or the United States. Not even one girl in a hundred was sexually molested by her own father. Fathers were the least likely of all men to molest a girl.

Much was made of a recent television special in the United States, broadcast simultaneously by two commercial networks and by public television, in which Oprah Winfrey interviewed half a dozen victims of sexual molestation in their childhood.

There is no reason to doubt the sincerity of Ms. Winfrey, who says that she herself was sexually abused as a child, or the sincerity of the people who appeared on the program. But sincerity does not make a show biz personality professionally qualified to analyze the statistics fed to her by activist organizations with an axe to grind.

No sane and decent person questions how despicable and harmful the sexual molestation of children is. What is open to question is how widespread it is and whether the kinds of policies proposed are likely to make matters better or worse, on net balance.

There are, after all, criminal laws on the books and there is no reason why degenerate parents cannot be treated like the criminals they are. But that is seldom what the promoters of child abuse hysteria have in mind.

The bottom line for too many of the zealots is more money and more authority for outsiders to intervene in families *before anything is proven.* Instead of locking up abusive parents, activists want them turned over to the "mental health" establishment, which will then have a government-supplied and government-financed clientele.

Like other groups who get their hands on the taxpayers' money by creating hysteria and promising miracles, the "mental health" establishment is long on claims and short on evidence. All too typically, research on the effectiveness of a California psychological program designed to help the families of abused children was conducted by the principal advocate of the program—and even he could find no real evidence that it worked.

With child abuse, as with the sexual harassment of women, the issue is not whether such things happen. All sorts of misdeeds happen, from jaywalking to genocide. The real question is whether it happened in particular cases—and what we are going to accept as evidence.

Children whose abuse was reported to the authorities have died from further abuse before the social agencies could get around to them, because these agencies were so bogged down in investigations of a deluge of unfounded charges against other people.

Government is a blunt instrument. Its policies should be limited to what blunt instruments can do. We gain nothing by pretending to know what we cannot know and to be able to do what we cannot do.

◆

SOCIAL DETERIORATION

SYDNEY, AUSTRALIA: Travel is supposed to be broadening, but sometimes you simply encounter the same things abroad that you have at home.

On a quiet Sunday afternoon in Sydney, my wife and I were strolling through an arcade and emerging into the street when we heard a woman shriek. A moment later, we saw a young man leap over a low railing and rush past us into the arcade. Right behind him came a young Asian woman in hot pursuit.

She climbed over the same railing, dropping her Christmas packages as she raced off after him.

"Thief! Thief!" she yelled frantically.

Turning around, we could see that he had a wallet in his hand—no doubt her wallet. As they both disappeared around a bend in the arcade, it didn't look like she was going to catch him.

Like many of the various kinds of parasites in Western societies, this young thief looked neither ragged nor hungry. He belonged to no visible minority and showed no apparent physical handicap. Indeed, the way he leaped over the railing suggested that he might do well in the Olympic hurdles.

Australia has so many welfare state benefits, for every conceivable purpose, that this young thief was hardly likely to be "driven to crime," as the intelligentsia like to put it. On the contrary, this maudlin attitude toward crime and other parasitic behavior probably has far more to do with the flourishing of vagrancy, welfare dependency, and criminality than any of the social "root causes" of crime so loftily talked about.

Australia and New Zealand share the same mushy attitudes that are prevalent throughout Western welfare states. "Crime can't happen in a community that cares," according to a poster in New Zealand. Isn't that a lovely sentiment? If only we were nicer to the bums, hoodlums and thieves, they would be nicer to us!

Not all societies buy this attitude. Japan doesn't. Criminals in Japan get punishment rather than sentimentality. In Tokyo's shopping districts, you can see great numbers of bicycles parked on the sidewalks—and not locked.

Singapore doesn't get maudlin over parasites either. Beggars get picked up and hustled out of town. They are brought back early in the morning on work details to clean up the streets.

There was a time when Western countries believed in punishing vagrancy instead of rewarding "homelessness." Criminals were held personally responsible for their crimes. Crime rates were far lower before we started listening to psycho-babble and handing over our hard-earned money to "service providers" in exchange for lofty rhetoric and vague promises.

Even low-income neighborhoods were far safer then. This was dramatized for me this past spring, during a visit to a high school in Harlem. When I mentioned that I used to walk my dog in the park across the street from the school, looks of horror came across the students' faces and the principal warned me not to do that today.

In an earlier era, a young married couple in my family used to lie down on the grass in that park on hot summer nights and go to sleep there, rather than stay in the hot tenements. Many other people did that, all over New York. Today you would be considered insane to try it.

It is not just different cultures that account for lower crime rates in places like Japan or Singapore. We once had far safer cities, including ghettoes, in the United States. That was when our social policies were based on actual experience of what worked—not on untested theories and lofty rhetoric.

Much of the social history of the Western world, over the past three decades, has been a history of replacing what worked with what sounded good. In area after area—crime, education, housing, race relations—the situation has gotten worse after the bright new theories were put into operation. The amazing thing is that this history of failure and disaster has neither discouraged the social engineers nor discredited them.

So what if our children's math scores dropped after the "new math" teaching methods were introduced, or teen-age pregnancy rates shot up after "sex education" became part of the curriculum, or crime rates soared after courts became more lenient, or homelessness reached new heights after federal, state, and local governments all got heavily involved in housing?

So what if all sorts of racial and ethnic animosities grew worse after new policies designed to produce multi-cultural harmony?

We may be entering an era when the greatest dangers to the survival of Western civilization will come from internal social deterioration. Other great civilizations have declined and collapsed. We may be the first, however, to sink slowly into the quagmire, still beaming from ear to ear in self-congratulation at how "innovative" we are in our social policies.

◆

WHAT'S NEWS?

"WHAT I DON'T KNOW ISN'T KNOWLEDGE," according to a satirical verse about Benjamin Jowett, the celebrated 19th century master of Balliol College. Today, what doesn't fit the ideological preconceptions of the media isn't news.

One of the most amazing facts about the American economy and society has remained as unknown in the media as the tree that fell in an empty forest. While talk about "the rich" and "the poor" abounds, recently released statistics from a Treasury Department study of income tax returns show that most Americans do not stay in the same part of the income distribution very long.

Among people whose incomes were in the bottom 20 percent in 1979, 86 percent were in some higher income bracket by 1988. In other words, only 14 percent of "the poor" were still in the bottom quintile a decade later. As people gain job experience, that shows up in the paycheck.

A surprising 15 percent had risen all the way to the top quintile by 1988, and 40 percent of "the poor" of 1979 were now in the top two quintiles.

This information, recently released by Congressman Richard Armey of Texas, did not make a ripple in the media, where income statistics as of a given moment are automatically assumed to show "class" differences, rather than the transient positions of individuals.

When only 14 percent of those whose incomes are in the bottom 20 percent remain there throughout a decade, this means that only 2.8 percent of the population studied were continuously "poor." In four out of the five quintiles, most people did not remain there until the end of the decade.

All the election-year rhetoric we hear about "the rich" and "the poor" is about people who, put together, add up to fewer than one American out of six.

Another recent study that has been as disregarded as the tree falling in the forest was a *Reader's Digest* poll about families and cultural values. First of all, it showed that 57 percent of Americans over the age of 24 were married couples with children—a sharp contrast with the "disappearance of the family" line so fashionable in the media.

The values of people who are married parents differ substantially from the values of those who follow the "alternative lifestyles" so much presented in the media.

Nearly three quarters of married parents say that mothers with small children should not work outside the home, unless it is economically necessary. Among singles and married couples without children, just over half take the opposite view, apparently thinking that career fulfillment and the like are sufficient reason for these mothers to take jobs, even without any economic necessity.

The cultural conservatism of married couples with children cuts across racial lines. Only 4 percent of black married parents favor the legalization of marijuana, compared with 18 percent of white married parents, and much higher percentages in other segments of the population.

This, incidentally, was not the first poll to show a strong conservative element within the black population, despite the almost uniformly liberal-left orientation of black "leaders" and intellectuals. That conservative political candidates have generally not been able to tap this element of the black population effectively has been due to historical factors—and to the ineptness of the conservative establishment.

In economic matters, as in cultural matters, large racial differences reflect the very different internal segmentations of the black and white populations, much more so than differences between blacks and whites of the same description. For example, black college-educated married couples overtook their white counterparts in income more than twenty years ago. The real problem is that there are far fewer blacks in this category and far more in categories that lead to poverty in both races, such as single mothers.

None of this makes a dent in the media's eye view of the world, where all differences between races are evidences of racism. Facts to the contrary are simply not news, as far as those who select and define news are concerned.

Nowhere is a one-sided view of what is news more prevalent than in media discussion of environmental issues. It is impossible to watch a nature program on television—public or commercial—without getting the Sierra Club political vision of the world, without even a hint that there are other viewpoints, much less facts that flatly contradict various claims.

Environmental hysteria is news, even when it comes from individuals and organizations whose past predictions have proved wrong, time and again, like Paul Ehrlich and the Worldwatch Institute. Scholarly studies puncturing the "overpopulation" myth, or climate experts who disagree with the "global warming" projections are not news.

If Benjamin Jowett were really the way he was depicted in satire, he would be right at home on television news programs.

---------------------------- ◆ ----------------------------

THE REAL ANITA HILL

A RECENTLY PUBLISHED BOOK may finally resolve one of the baffling puzzles of our times—whether Clarence Thomas or Anita Hill was lying in their much-publicized appearances before the Senate Judiciary Committee. At that time, it was basically a question of his word against hers. That is no longer the case.

After reading David Brock's carefully researched book, *The Real Anita Hill*, those who wish to believe Professor Hill will have to believe that a small army of other people have lied when they flatly contradicted many parts of her story. These include people from every place where she has worked since graduating from law school, her students at two different universities, and F.B.I. agents who interviewed her, among others.

Although the contents of this book are dynamite, there is no sensationalism, no strident political editorializing, no rhetorical flourishes. There is only the slow but steady build-up of facts and careful analysis of claims and arguments on both sides of the Hill-Thomas controversy. But, in the end, it adds up to a complete devastation of the testimony—and the media image—of Anita Hill.

In a controversy about something that is supposed to have happened when there were no witnesses present, the character and credibility of the people involved is crucial. But although Clarence Thomas' life and character have been gone over with a microscope, much less has been known about the life and character of Anita Hill—until this book.

The picture that emerges is not a pretty picture, but it is documented to the hilt and it comes from innumerable sources. The consistency of that picture makes it hard to ignore or dismiss.

One of the points of controversy has been Anita Hill's reasons for following Clarence Thomas from the Department of Education to the Equal Employment Opportunity Commission, if he behaved in the vile manner she described. She said that she was afraid of losing her job—but people who worked with her at the time said that she was well aware that her job was safe.

The man who replaced Clarence Thomas at the Department of Education, Harry Singleton, went further. "I talked to Anita a number of times," he said. Because Thomas was taking other aides with him to E.E.O.C., "I didn't want to be left without any staff, so I asked Anita if she was going to stay. I told her I would like her to stay. But she said, 'Oh no, I'm going with Clarence.' She was lying to the committee.'"

On a personal level, the picture of Clarence Thomas relentlessly pursuing Anita Hill is turned upside down by a number of people who knew her at the time, who picture her as trying to get closer to him, both at the office and after work.

One of the anecdotes from that period concerns Anita Hill's complaints about her slow social life in general, and in particular Clarence Thomas' failure to respond to her. On one occasion, when he dropped her off in his car, on his way home from work, she invited him inside and then offered him a glass of wine, which he declined. Instead, they talked at length about politics, Clarence's grandfather, and Ronald Reagan—none of which was apparently what Anita had in mind.

What seems painfully clear from this book is that Clarence Thomas never really understood Anita Hill's feelings toward him, either during the early period when she was trying to develop a social relationship with him or at the end of her stay at the E.E.O.C., when she was bitter at having failed to get a promotion she was seeking. Other people saw the situation for what it was, and at least one tried to warn him about her growing hostility toward him.

Nevertheless, just a couple of months before Anita Hill's sensational charges were made, Judge Thomas was telling Justice Department officials where they could contact her, to get her to appear as a witness in his behalf at the confirmation hearings. He was completely blindsided by her allegations.

Perhaps the ugliest revelations about the character and personality of Anita Hill concern her treatment of her students after she became a law professor. Some of these students are quoted concerning her combination of mistreatment of male students and her sexual innuendoes with them—including putting pubic hairs in their exam booklets and referring to the porn star Long Dong Silver.

The big question now is whether so many people have such a vested interest in Anita Hill as a politically useful symbol that they will seek to kill this book, either by silence or misrepresentation.

---------------------◆---------------------

THE CHUMP SOCIETY

PARIS HAS MANY FOREIGNERS—Vietnamese refugees, Africans, people from the Middle East, and others. Many of these people work as maids, clerks, policemen or in other occupations. The Japanese own one of the big hotels on the Left Bank.

But when you see beggars on the street, they are almost always Frenchmen—usually young and healthy looking. Sometimes they carry a simple sign: *"J'ai faim"* ("I am hungry").

It is no secret that human beings get hungry every day. What is news is that we now have whole classes of people who think it is somebody else's responsibility to get them food. That is the tragic message about the deterioration of values, not only in France, but in Western society.

In California, there are likewise a variety of races and nationalities. Mexican Americans are especially numerous. But you can go for years without seeing a Mexican American begging in the streets.

In San Francisco or Los Angeles, as in Paris, the beggar is often young, white, and healthy looking. Sometimes he is black. But almost never is he Mexican.

The argument for the welfare state is that the "victims" of "society" do not have the money, the education, or the opportunity to take care of themselves. But groups who are not yet used to the welfare state often come into the country destitute, ill-educated, barely speaking the language, and yet seem to find jobs pretty quickly.

It is the people who were born and raised in the welfare state atmosphere who seem to have great difficulty finding jobs. Not only does the government support such individuals. So do the people who pass on the street, dropping coins and bills into their cups.

Over the years, we have been called an affluent society, a post-industrial society, and all kinds of other societies. But many of the intractable problems we face come from the fact that we have become a chump society.

What makes us a chump society is our refusal to recognize that there is no predestined amount of poverty or homelessness—that our policies are creating more of both by subsidizing them, just as we create agricultural surpluses by subsidizing farming. You can have as much poverty as you are willing to pay for.

The big argument for the welfare state is that we must establish some minimum standard of living for all members of our community or family. "Community" is a great word and a great concept. So is "family." But being a member of either is not a one-way street. Members pay their dues and obey the rules. Chumps plus parasites do not add up to a family.

Far from creating a greater sense of community, the welfare state has emboldened the parasites against the chumps. They demand as "rights" more of what other people have worked for. Parasites are indignant—and deep-thinkers are indignant for them—at any suggestion that they change their "life style" so as to support themselves.

One of the signs of a deteriorating sense of community is vandalism against public property—which has never been greater than during this era of "caring" for all "members" of the "community." Parasites know that they are not members of the community. What respect can they be expected to have for a community that lets them walk all over it? Nobody respects a chump.

PART II
THE WORLD SCENE

◆

INDIA'S ECONOMY

BOMBAY: India is a classic Third World country and Western intellectuals have the classic illusions, emotions, and blind spots about it.

There is no illusion about the poverty of India, or about the hard fact that more than half its people are illiterate. The fallacy of the intellectuals, and of political policies influenced by them, is the belief that sending money to the Indian government as foreign aid, and shipping Western brainpower to India as "experts," is the answer.

India has produced vast amounts of trained brainpower, including scientific, business and financial skills. But the heavy-handed control of the economy by the Indian government stifles the skills and talents already in the country, and often drives them overseas, where Indians flourish.

More than one-fourth of all the hotels and motels in the United States are owned by people from India. About one-tenth of all anesthesiologists in American hospitals are from India. The average income of people from India living in the United States is significantly higher than that of the average American.

The United States is by no means unique in receiving India's skills and capital. Indians own most of what is worth owning in Fiji—a fact not unrelated to the recent military coup by the Fijian army. Indians created much of the modern economy of several nations in East Africa, where the rupee was once the prevalent currency. Indians are doing well in Britain and Trinidad, among other places.

Surely poverty-stricken India could use some of the vast supply of skills and capital which its people are putting to use all around the world. And surely both cultural attractions and economic forces would draw some of that talent home if the stifling economic regulation maintained by the government of India did not create an impossible situation.

Things that American businessmen do freely on their own initiative require all kinds of government approval in India. The delays, uncertainties, and inefficiencies this introduces into every economic activity—from the simplest to the most complex—make it harder to produce the very output needed to raise India's standard of living.

Even to use more electricity, a Bombay businessman has had to submit reports to the government. Moreover, he knew that government approval might not be given if his business decisions or personal demeanor did not meet the approval of the bureaucrats who second-guess him. He had to conduct his business, not in the most efficient way, but in a way that would pass muster politically.

India is not unusual among Third World countries in having suffocating government control of the economy. Many other Third World countries also have much educated, entrepreneurial, and scientific talent overseas, where that talent is adding to the prosperity of other nations.

Politics is the crucial obstacle to retaining such much-needed talent at home. To allow scarce and valuable skills a free hand is to risk having such skills become so highly rewarded as to provoke envy—a powerful and dangerous political force.

Part of such envy is natural, but much of it is hyped by intellectuals and politicians—both of whom get more worked up by how the pie is sliced than by how big a pie it is. Spectacular increases in output have occurred in some countries that deregulated their economies, as Sri Lanka did about a decade ago. But, even if everyone benefits, there can still be hell to pay politically, if some group benefits a little more than another.

This dog-in-the-manger political approach to the economy has much to do with governments' excessive regulation. In loftier circles, it is known as "social justice."

So-called "social justice" should never be confused with humanitarianism. From a humanitarian viewpoint, it is infinitely more important to have a prospering economy, in which the great masses of the people are beyond the reach of hunger and malnutrition, and beyond the reach of poverty-related diseases, than to stifle a relative handful of specially skilled or talented people who might be envied. But denouncing "disparities" and "inequities" is where it's at politically, not only in India, but in much of the world.

Countries that already had flourishing economies before the "social justice" crusade struck are often able to absorb its costs because of their general affluence. But this lofty talk and stultifying reality are a much heavier burden for India.

Under these circumstances, the problem with foreign aid is that it bails out the very governments responsible for holding back development. Such donations to governments, whether open or hidden as "soft loans," are also unnecessary, because far larger sums of capital are available in the world market. Stock exchanges, banks, and all sorts of other institutional and individual investors send hundreds of billions of dollars overseas all the time.

The difference between these massive international transfers of capital and foreign aid is that private investors usually require some prospect that their investments will actually pan out. But foreign aid will sponsor all sorts of government boondoggles—including bailouts from debts caused by previous boondoggles.

Naturally, Third World governments prefer foreign aid, even if their economies could get more capital from private investors by relaxing the grip of politicians. Foreign aid goes into the hands of politicians, to hand out as favors—and some of it often ends up in their own pockets.

If the West truly wants to improve the standard of living of Third World peoples, it will stop bankrolling boondoggles and let countries like India rely on the abundant supply of capital available for projects with some real prospects of being productive.

◆

CHINA'S BIRTH CONTROL

A CHILLING STORY OUT OF CHINA shows the grim and brutal consequences of grand ideological visions. In addition to the general Communist vision of a government-controlled economy and society, the so-called People's Republic of China has also become determined to control the number of children each family has.

One couple was fined more than they earn in a year for having two "unauthorized" births above the officially allotted one-per-family, according to a recent report in *The Wall Street Journal*. Moreover, local Communist officials stand to have their pay cut if people under their jurisdiction have more children than the government allows. Under these conditions, the pressures against women who want to have more children are unrelenting.

Providing "access" to birth-control information or devices is not the issue in China (or in most other countries). China has what birth-control pushers really want—the ability to propagandize and pressure people into doing what the anointed have decided needs doing. In China, people can be furloughed from their jobs, or their pay can be cut, for having more than the government-allotted number of children.

Dossiers are kept on every couple, and women's individual menstrual cycles are charted in these government dossiers. Not only is Big Brother watching you; big sister is watching even more closely. Female officials "conduct spot checks in the home to make sure intrauterine devices are still in place."

Ugly as all this is, it is the logical consequence of the vision of the anointed. Once you buy the notion that the intellectually superior and the morally anointed should take "leadership" in "public service" and "make a difference" by using government power to force others into a preconceived pattern, this is where that road ends. Some may not have the stomach to follow the road that far, but this is where it leads. Where power and glory are to be had from following the logic of the vision, it is only a matter of time before those who are squeamish are replaced by those who are not squeamish.

The great irony is that the anointed themselves often have no solid basis for the draconian policies they impose on the masses. Often their basis is nothing more than fashionable speculation mixed with ideological fervor and blind self-righteousness. The dogma that "overpopulation" causes poverty is a classic example.

There are sparsely populated and prosperous countries like the United States, but Ethiopia has almost the identical number of people per square mile as the U.S. and is desperately poor. China is more densely populated and poor, but Japan and West Germany are even more densely populated and very prosperous. Anyone who takes the trouble to look up the statistics can find almost any population density among either rich countries or poor countries.

It is not population but productivity that determines whether nations are rich or poor. If there were only three people on the whole planet, and they produced just enough for two to live on, they would be in big trouble. By the same token, if there were 10 times as many people as there are today, and they produced 20 times the output, their standard of living would be twice as high as ours. History shows that our standard of living is far higher than people enjoyed in past ages, when the world's population was only a fraction of what it is now.

Brutal birth-control methods, such as those in China, do not produce as low birth-rates as those in the United States or Western Europe, where people are free to do as they wish. But brutal methods, and the sense of desperate urgency on which they are based, all enhance the power and the egos of the anointed.

Even the reporter for the *Wall Street Journal* got sucked into the notion that the Chinese Communists are fighting some desperate battle against "overpopulation." The predictions of "some international demographers" are cited, along with the statistic that "China had to import about 15 million tons of grain last year."

A book could easily be filled with the history of grossly wrong predictions by demographers. Half a century ago, the big hysteria was that population growth in the West was so slow that economic decline would set in—all this on the eve of a baby boom and an economic boom. More recently Paul Ehrlich's book, *The Population Bomb*, spread the opposite hysteria of overpopulation—at a time when birth rates in the U.S. were dropping so sharply that obstetricians, gynecologists, and toy manufacturers were all suffering an economic pinch.

As for importing grain, that has often happened in Communist countries whose stifling control of agriculture hurts productivity, even when these countries have far less population density than China. But the mindset that stifles agriculture is all too ready to believe that the answer to its bad consequences is to stifle people.

The vision of the anointed extends far beyond Communist countries, though in other countries it has to contend with other visions, and even its own devotees are inhibited by such things as the Judeo-Christian tradition, in which the individual has both responsibility and rights. But, to the extent that the vision of the anointed is pervasive—as it is among intellectuals—we are moving further in the direction of government control of more and more of our lives. What is happening in China is the logical end of that process.

◆

BILINGUALISM IN SINGAPORE

SINGAPORE: Bilingual education is government policy in Singapore, as it is in the United States. The difference is that Singapore is serious about having its students learn two languages. In the United States, "bilingualism" is just one of many loose and misleading expressions concealing a hidden agenda of ideologues and hustlers.

American "bilingualism" too often means simply teaching students in the language spoken at home, alienating them from English and from their English-speaking classmates. Teaching children in an educational ghetto will not help prepare them for a future life in American society. But it will help provide current jobs for ethnic teachers, a constituency for ethnic "leaders" and an opportunity for anti-American indoctrination in the schools.

Singapore is neither big enough nor rich enough to afford to be as foolish about education as the United States. Singapore has overcome many handicaps to become a prosperous, clean and very attractive city-state in tropical Southeast Asia. An independent nation, it is smaller than Los Angeles but is one of the great ports of the world and one of the economic success stories of Asia.

The population of Singapore is approximately two-thirds Chinese and they speak a variety of Chinese dialects. Large numbers of Malays in Singapore speak the Malay language and Singapore's Indian population speaks languages or dialects from India.

There are all the ingredients here for a tower of Babel or for the kind of bitter disputes over language policy which have plagued Canada, Belgium, India and Sri Lanka, among others. Yet the Singapore government has avoided both problems with a bilingual policy that means what it says—learning two languages. Each Singapore student must learn to speak English—correctly— and to speak his or her own ethnic language, also correctly.

There is no sentimental nonsense in Singapore about one way of talking being just as good as another. Far from encouraging dialects, as "black English," for example, is encouraged in some places in the United States, Singapore insists that Chinese students learn to speak standard Mandarin Chinese, not the various dialects spoken in their homes.

Many Chinese students are finding Mandarin Chinese a tough language to master. Yet Singapore's Prime Minister, Lee Kuan Yew, insists that they must learn it. Speaking himself in Mandarin Chinese, he acknowledged the difficulties but insisted on a standard language so that Chinese people in Singapore can understand each other's speech.

Chinese writing is not phonetic. So, while literate Chinese may all understand the meaning of a given symbol, their verbal statement of the same idea would differ greatly according to their respective dialects—just as a Frenchman, a German, and a Russian would understand the same thing by the number 2,315 but would say it in entirely different ways.

In Singapore, the goal is to get the Chinese to be able to speak to each other in mutually understandable ways in Mandarin, and for all Singaporeans to be able to communicate with each other in English. "Singaporeans have to master English to make a living," Prime Minister Lee said, recognizing his country's economic dependence on its role as a world port and a world financial center.

When Singapore became an independent nation a quarter of a century ago, it had no assurance of surviving, much less thriving as it has. What it has achieved under difficult conditions has many lessons for other countries, not only in the Third World, but in North America as well. Singapore's practical approach to language policy is well worth thinking about.

Languages serve a practical, common-sense purpose—communicating with other people. Language policies have to be judged in the light of that basic reality. A language or dialect that severely restricts how many people you can communicate with is a great handicap, no matter what its merits may be, compared to other languages.

Spanish may be a language of great beauty and subtlety, but if you live in an English-speaking country like the United States, you cannot use it to communicate with as many people as you can reach in English. If you cannot communicate well with employers, you may not get the job and if you cannot communicate well in an emergency with doctors, paramedics, or firemen, you could lose your life.

English is the most widely spoken language on earth. Singapore's bilingual policy puts its people in communication with a billion other people on this planet who speak English. What is called "bilingualism," in the United States is too often an escape from having to master English—and paints people into a corner for life.

◆

BEGGARS IN PARIS

PARIS: Travel is supposed to be broadening but sometimes it is just depressing—especially when you see the same signs of degeneration overseas that you see at home.

One of these signs, in Paris as in London or New York, are the sophisticated modern beggars. These are not your old-fashioned, ragged, grizzled, or hang-dog-looking beggars. These are your new, clean, young, and able-bodied beggars. They are people who look just like everybody else—except when they have their hands out.

I encountered four beggars in less than half an hour of travelling on the Paris subway. The first was an upbeat and self-confident young woman who made a little speech in the subway car as it was moving between stations. My French was not good enough to pick up all that she was saying, but the bottom line was that she wanted something to eat.

Various people offered her money and, as she moved past to get it, I noticed that her handbag seemed rather stylish. She said "Merci" and was off to another car to put on the same show.

Later, there was another beggar next to the exit of the subway station where I got off. He was too fat to be able to say that he was hungry, with any credibility. However, he carried a sign saying that he was out of work. Obviously, you couldn't be standing around begging in a subway station if you had a job to go to. But he may be taking home more money this way.

When I returned to the subway to go back to my hotel, there was a healthy-looking young fellow holding a sign announcing that he was unemployed. He seemed surprised—and a little indignant—that a bunch of us walked right past him without offering anything. If everyone was this cold-hearted, he might have to resort to getting a job.

The fourth beggar was the first one with any plausibility. She was elderly, sitting down, and had a cotton patch over one eye. If she had been the only beggar I had seen all day, I probably would have given her something. But, clearly, begging has become a way of life in Paris, as in many other cities of the Western world.

One of the classic scenes of our times occurred a few weeks ago on the streets of San Francisco. A middle-aged black woman, dressed in no way that would suggest affluence, paused to open her pocket book to give some money to an able-bodied white man who was begging there. It was yet another sign of how we have all been brain-washed.

It is right that those of us who have been more fortunate should feel gratitude for our blessings and try to share those blessings in some way. But you don't show gratitude by undermining the very society that made your good fortune possible. There are a thousand worthy endeavors that need support. But no society needs more parasites.

The money absorbed by those parasites is the least of the problems. Between the welfare state and thoughtless handouts on the streets, a whole class of people is emerging—unwilling to work and contemptuous of the society that feeds them. There are innumerable signs of this contempt, from "aggressive pan-handling" to urinating in public places.

Has anyone noticed how many hideous crimes turn out to have been committed by someone described as "a drifter"? Can you support an ever-growing class of people leading dissolute and irresponsible lives and not expect more crime? When a "drifter" killed innocent schoolchildren in California not long ago with a semi-automatic weapon, the political answer was to ban semi-automatic weapons—and do nothing about drifters.

Travel is still broadening, to some extent. The cultural riches of Paris are not the same as those of London or New York. What is peculiar to each of these cities reflects what their various societies have contributed to the development of Western civilization. What they have in common today too often reflects the degeneration that threatens the long-run survival of that civilization.

It is not just a large and growing class of vagrants and criminals that is common in Western societies. Western nations also have in common another large and growing class that lives by its wits—intellectuals and pseudo-intellectuals. Through the media and academia, they generate many of the attitudes and theories that create acceptance of parasites, who are depicted as "victims" of "society."

In reality, it is these parasites who are victimizing society daily—and undermining the foundations of civilization in the long run.

◆

WESTERN CIVILIZATION UNDER SIEGE

WESTERN CIVILIZATION HAS SURVIVED the invasions of Genghis Khan from the East, the Ottoman Empire from the South, and two world wars originating from within. But whether it will survive its own intellectuals is much more doubtful.

The battlefront is everywhere, but especially where the young are being taught—from the elementary school to the university. The sins of the human race are being taught to them as the special depravities of the United States or of Western civilization.

Deep thinkers like to talk about such things as the oppression of women in Western society—when in fact women have had a much lower position in Islamic cultures, for example, and girl babies were often routinely killed in parts of Asia. It was a Western nation—Britain—which put an end to the burning of widows alive on their husbands' funeral pyres in India.

Slavery is of course the trump card of critics of Western civilization. But the tragic fact is that this abomination has existed on every continent inhabited by man. The pyramids were built by slaves, long before Columbus discovered America, and human beings were bought and sold for centuries in Asia as well. Slavery existed in both North and South America before the first white man set foot in the Western Hemisphere.

Hard and painful as it is to realize today, leading moralists in many lands and in many centuries saw nothing wrong with slavery. It was precisely in the West—notably in England—that a moral revulsion against slavery and a movement to stamp it out everywhere developed in the late eighteenth century.

Only the unchallenged might of the British navy, patrolling the waters off Africa for decades in the early nineteenth century, brought the shipment of slaves to the Western Hemisphere to an end. The Czarist regime in Russia, though despotic by Western standards, stamped out slavery among Central Asians in its domains. The efforts of many Western powers to stop slavery within their empires and spheres of influence in Africa and the Middle East continued on well into the twentieth century, over bitter opposition by Arabs and Africans alike.

The West must accept its share of the blame for participating in the exploitation and degradation of human beings, but that is very different from taking the rap for everybody else—or allowing phoney history to poison its own children's minds today.

Gross double standards in judging Western and non-Western cultures have become so commonplace among intellectuals that few seem to notice it any more. Tragedies and injustices common to the human species around the world are referred to as flaws in "our society." Every ugly incident, however isolated, is immediately magnified in the media, and often treasured for years afterward, as something to be resurrected whenever anyone dares to say anything good about America or Western society.

Meanwhile, many of the same intellectuals gush over foreign tyrants and brush aside their bloody oppression as mere stages on the road to a glowing future. At the height of Mao's "cultural revolution" in China—an orgy of intolerant repressions, terror, public humiliations and mass killings—Western intellectuals flocked to China and returned to say how wonderful it all was. Mao's little red book of sayings was a hot item in campus bookstores while he subjugated one-fourth of the human race and made them pawns and guinea pigs for his visions.

Abortions forcibly imposed on Chinese women nearing time to give birth aroused nothing like the indignation which our intellectuals express when racial slurs are uttered during a teenage brawl in New York. Horrors imposed by numerous authorities carrying out government policies in China are called regrettable "excesses" of "local officials," while any isolated assassin in the United States is said to represent a pervasive "sickness" of American society.

Those who habitually use such double standards are seldom poor or people with any personal reason for being embittered. Often they are some of the most fortunate and pampered people in Western society, including both highly paid media intellectuals and academics with soft schedules and numerous perks. Why these should be among the most venomous critics of the West—and the most blindly one-sided—is no doubt a long and complex story. However, spoiled brats have seldom been noted for their gratitude.

♦

TESTING INTELLIGENCE

DUNEDIN, NEW ZEALAND: To an American, the city of Dunedin, in southern New Zealand, may seem to be about as far away as you can get on this planet. Yet, in this isolated little port on the Pacific, there is an expatriate American whose research has worldwide significance. He is Professor James R. Flynn, of Otago University, who is conducting a global study of how well various peoples do on mental tests.

This controversial and potentially explosive subject is handled by Professor Flynn with great scholarly care, and with penetrating insight into the very complicated issues involved. His statistics cover more than a dozen countries, stretching from Britain to Japan to the United States to New Zealand.

Jim Flynn is not just a numbers-cruncher, however. He knows the ins and outs of the many different I.Q. tests and what the mysterious scores that come out of them mean—and don't mean. Why is all this important? Because his analysis gives us clues as to what intelligence itself is and what differences in results on "intelligence tests" mean.

Many of the early pioneers in mental testing were convinced from the outset that intelligence was inherited. From this they concluded that the government should follow policies designed to perpetuate the most intelligent individuals and races, and to see that the least intelligent faded away to extinction. If you just let nature take its course, they reasoned, the least intelligent people would tend to have the largest families and become a growing proportion of the population, thereby lowering the average intelligence of nations and of the human species in general.

Professor Jim Flynn's worldwide research shows that, contrary to this reasoning and these predictions, the average mental test performance has risen by large amounts over the past few generations. Whole nations have had their scores rise by more than the current I.Q. difference between blacks and whites, for example. This enormously important fact is obscured by the way I.Q. scores are figured.

By definition, the average I.Q. is 100. If the average person answers 52 questions correctly on a given I.Q. test, then 52 right answers becomes an I.Q. of 100. Twenty years later, if the average person answers 65 questions correctly, then 65 right answers becomes an I.Q. of 100. Anybody who answers 52 questions correctly now may end up with an I.Q. in the 80s.

What Professor Flynn's research shows is that more and more people are answering more and more I.Q. test questions correctly, in countries around the world. Only relatively briefly do nations' I.Q.s rise, however, because the new number of correct answers soon becomes the new norm for an I.Q. of 100.

These large, but concealed, improvements in I.Q. test performance around the world shoot down many ideas about intelligence. The idea of a genetically fixed intelligence is hard to believe, in the wake of major changes in I.Q. test performance from one generation to the next. Flynn even questions whether I.Q. tests really measure intelligence.

The number of people who answer enough questions correctly to be considered "geniuses" by the original I.Q. standards has gone up by leaps and bounds. Yet we see no corresponding increase in the kind of people who could be compared to Beethoven, Einstein, or Galileo. The ability to answer a lot of routine questions rapidly does not add up to genius.

It's not that I.Q. tests or other mental tests "don't mean anything." They mean a lot in some contexts and not much in others.

Even tests of mere information can be very useful, if that information is needed to pursue some educational goal or career goal. Tests of reasoning ability, or facility with language or mathematics, may also be valuable, depending on what these tests are used for.

Mental tests cannot be simply waved aside as "irrelevant," as some have tried to do, especially since the 1960s. Many able minority students, for example, have been needlessly sacrificed by being thrown into college situations where they had little or no chance of surviving academically, because they were grossly mismatched with an institution whose other students had far higher Scholastic Aptitude Test scores. It is little short of a crime to have youngsters flunking out of high-pressure institutions, when they could graduate with honors from most American colleges.

Mental tests need to be looked at with common sense—not with awe or with sweeping dismissals. Professor Jim Flynn's research should help us all to see these tests in perspective.

◆

THE MINDSET OF MUNICH

HALF A CENTURY AGO—on September 29, 1938—the Western democracies made the biggest and most tragic blunder of the twentieth century, one that almost cost them their existence. On that day, the leaders of Britain, France, Germany, and Italy met in Munich to reach an agreement giving Germany some adjacent territory in Czechoslovakia.

This little transfer of land, whose inhabitants were mostly German, may seem today like a small thing—as it seemed at the time like a small price to pay for peace. The Germans in the Czech borderlands had for months been clamoring and rioting to be reunited with their fatherland and Hitler was threatening to send in troops to "liberate" them.

Seen in this light—as a trade of "land for peace"—it looked like a good deal. Under pressure from Britain and France, Czechoslovakia accepted it.

The tragedy was in the whole misconception that saw things in this light—as an isolated episode over grievances with indigenous roots, a "problem" to be "solved." The issue was never whether Germans could rejoin Gemany. The issue was whether they could take Czechoslovakia's land and border defenses with them.

Once the heavily fortified and mountainous region of Czechoslovakia was gone, the rest of the country was defenseless against the Nazi army. So was much of the rest of eastern Europe. Together with Nazi acquisition of Czech munitions factories in the area, this shifted the whole balance of power on the continent of Europe in Hitler's favor and against Britain and France.

Yet the Western "leaders" spoke of it as if it were just a matter of letting some Germans go home. It was the greatest of all deceptions, self-deception.

The Czech crisis was only one in a series of carefully graduated steps by which Hitler advanced his goal of Nazi domination of Europe, and then of the world. "There is no safety for honest men but by believing all possible evil of evil men," Edmund Burke wrote, back in the eighteenth century. But the twentieth-century mind finds it hard to accept the very concept of deliberately chosen, calculated evil—whether among delinquents and criminals or totalitarian dictators.

During the Munich era, British Prime Minister Neville Chamberlain exemplified the twentieth-century mindset in democratic societies. He spoke repeatedly of "misunderstandings" and "suspicions" among nations as the great dangers to peace—dangers to be dissipated by "personal contacts" among leaders of potentially hostile nations. Summit meetings are the logical consequence of this mindset and Chamberlain, more than anyone else, can be considered the inventor of summit meetings.

Chamberlain represented not simply a party or a policy of the moment, but the mindset of an age. In that mindset, wars grow out of a lack of understanding, hostile passions, or "arms races," rather than out of deliberately calculated evil. Summits, soft words, and concessions make sense, if this is your conception of the world. But directly opposite policies would be needed to deal with deliberate evil—military deterrents, for example.

Chamberlain was forever deploring the money spent on military weapons. The weapons themselves were viewed as the enemy, much as they are today.

Chamberlain was not alone. Many British intellectuals and politicians argued that it was "hopeless" to try to stop bombers with anti-aircraft guns and interceptor fighter planes. In their vision, neither defense nor deterrence was possible. That left only appeasement or capitulation as alternatives. All this was believed with great conviction—and with great condescension toward anyone who dared to think differently.

When Winston Churchill rose in Parliament to criticize the Munich agreement and the whole philosophy behind it, he was repeatedly interrupted by cries of derision from other members of Parliament—from his own party as well as the opposition. Churchill was also denounced and ridiculed in the press.

Why was Munich important? Immediately it was important because it gave the Nazis important strategic advantages, without their having to fire a shot or lose a soldier. The bigger and longer run importance of Munich was that it convinced Hitler that the West was gutless, that it was safe for him to begin open aggression.

It also demonstrated for future aggressors how easy it is to deceive Western democracies with pretty words—no matter how ugly the reality. The Soviets have learned that lesson well.

World War II was a near thing. For nearly three years, Germany and Japan won an almost unbroken series of devastating victories. France fell in only six weeks of fighting and the smaller nations of Europe were overwhelmed in a matter of days. In the Far East, once Japan crippled the American fleet at Pearl Harbor, Japanese forces swept swiftly across thousands of miles of conquered lands, until they were within striking distance of Australia. All that saved Britain was accomplishing the "impossible" task of stopping bombers with anti-aircraft fire and interceptor fighter planes.

Eventually, the superior industrial capacity of the West turned the tide, as even the Russians fought with Western equipment. But today, in a nuclear war, superior industrial capacity will not have time to matter. The only time it can matter is beforehand—and only if it is used to build up a defense and a deterrence that will prevent a nuclear war from being launched in the first place.

The only thing that prevents us from maintaining deterrence is the mindset of Munich. This time it may indeed prove fatal.

$$\blacklozenge$$

ALL OVER THE MAP

STRIKE, IF YOU MUST, this old gray head but touch not the Mercator Projection!

What is a Mercator Projection, that it would call forth this melodramatic defense? Mercator was a 16th century map-maker, who projected a certain kind of map for use by navigators. It is still often seen on walls as a map of the world.

Recently, the Mercator Projection has come under ideological attack for the way it distorts the land areas of the world. Deep thinkers find it sinister, if not racist.

Like any map, the Mercator Projection cannot accurately represent a three-dimensional planet on a flat piece of paper. Maps can be projected different ways for different purposes, so they are all inaccurate in different ways, in order to be accurate in the particular way that matters for their purposes.

Since Mercator's map has been used for navigation, rather than for buying real estate, it gets the directions right at the expense of distorting the areas.

If you head straight for the top of a map which is a Mercator Projection, you are heading due north. Turn at a right angle and you are heading due east. On the other hand, Greenland is bigger than Australia on a Mercator Projection—just the opposite of the reality.

The distortions between Greenland and Australia don't worry the deep thinkers. What has them full of righteous indignation is the distortion between tropical continents and northern hemisphere continents like Europe and North America.

Because areas near the equator are represented as smaller than they really are, relative to countries and continents nearer the poles, that means that tropical Third World countries and continents look smaller, while Europe and North America look larger than they really are on a Mercator Projection.

The Mercator Projection thus represents "the self-conceit of the white man," according to one deep thinker, who published his own "egalitarian map" of the world. Another deep thinker said that the Mercator Projection may have exacerbated the Cold War, by making the Soviet Union look like "a huge looming red mass on the map."

It is reassuring that some people, for whom indignation is a way of life, have to go to such extremes to find something to be indignant about. However, I have a soft spot in my heart for the Mercator Projection, going all the way back to the time when I was a kid in the ninth grade.

Our English teacher made each of us get up in front of the class to give brief public speeches. On the day when my talk was due, I couldn't think of anything. I was desperately asking around among my classmates for suggestions before class.

Most were too busy working on their notes for their own speeches. But even those who offered suggestions didn't come up with anything worthwhile.

When the dreaded moment came, I went up to the front of the room and began: "My topic for today is _____" with no idea how that sentence would end.

I paused and turned in despair toward the side wall. There on the wall was a map of the world and the first words on it that struck me were—you guessed it—"Mercator Projection."

"_____ is the Mercator Projection," I said. "There happens to be one over here on the wall," I added, pointing.

My classmates watched tensely, because they had no more idea what I was going to say next than I did. I went into the different kinds of maps and what they were used for, and finally my time was up.

As I started to head back to my seat, the teacher told me to stay there. She came over, put her hand on my shoulder, and said to the class: "Now that was a model of how a speech should be made."

They were as dumbfounded as I was.

"First of all," she said, "notice that he had studied his subject so thoroughly that he didn't even need notes."

My classmates were struggling to keep from cracking up.

"Notice too," the teacher said, "how he paused after each statement to let it sink in, instead of just rushing along helter-skelter."

Some of my classmates took deep breaths.

"That was a very effective technique," she continued, "for I could see how he had the complete attention of the audience."

Somehow, none of us burst out laughing and all was well that ended well.

Anyhow, don't mess with the Mercator Projection. It rescued me when I needed it, and now it's time for me to return the favor.

◆

DESPOTISM IN RETREAT

AS THE LAST DECADE to the twentieth century begins, freedom seems to have the tide running in its favor, in many parts of the world. However, the struggle between freedom and despotism has gone on for too many centuries, in too many ways, and in too many places, for us to say that it is now over.

What may be beginning a decline toward extinction is one particular kind of despotism. The state-run Utopia—either Communist or Fascist—has had its meteoric rise and fall in the twentieth century. The intellectual elite, more so than the masses, have cheered loudly for one form of totalitarianism or another through much of this century.

Around a small solid core of fanatical zealots for Communism, Fascism, and the like, there has been a far wider gray zone of sympathetic fellow-travellers, including such luminaries as George Bernard Shaw, Thorstein Veblen, and many others. Still deeper in the shadows were those in Britain and America who became traitors to the freest countries in the world, in order to pass the most dangerous military secrets of the nuclear age to the worst despotism on earth, Stalin's U.S.S.R. Despotism can have an incredibly strong appeal, and its dangers will not be understood until that fact is faced.

Long before the political despotisms of this century appeared, there were religious despotisms that spread persecution and warfare across vast regions of the world. The desire to order other people around, and make them conform to one's own vision, takes many forms.

Those worshippers of imposed grand schemes who lack the stomach for the tortures of the Inquisition, or the concentration camps of twentieth century totalitarianism, have often embraced socialism as the form of control from the top down that we should have. Only within the past decade has this milder form of idealistic despotism begun to retreat, as the demonstrated benefits of freeing markets from political control won converts around the world, including socialist governments.

During the twentieth century, Fascism in Italy, Nazism in Germany, and

Communism in Russia, China, and elsewhere have all discredited themselves as ideals that spawned horrors in practice. For all but a handful of true believers, largely concentrated in the ivory towers of academe, such sweeping systems of despotism are dead morally and intellectually, however danger- ously alive they may be in some well-armed governments.

While the intellectual and moral battle against political despotism has gone in favor of freedom, the guerilla war may continue for generations to come. Few today dare to advocate sweeping forms of despotism as the road to Utopia, but many are advocating single-issue policies that, put together, add up to despotism. There is no way that the agendas of the environmental extremists, feminist radicals, "affirmative action" zealots, "industrial policy" promoters, and many others, can all be carried out without taking away freedom on the instalment plan.

The great danger, as the twentieth century nears its close and a new century looms ahead, is that freedom will be bled to death for the sake of innumerable "causes" and the narrow-minded zealots who push them— heedless of any other considerations, including the truth. The media's ea- gerness to jump on bandwagons, and to whoop it up for any half-baked idea or hysteria that will stir up excitement, serves to amplify the influence of single-issue fanatics.

The fight to preserve freedom into the twenty-first century may well depend on our ability to stay the course against incessant guerilla warfare like this.

PART III
THE ECONOMIC SCENE

◆

"RICH" AND "POOR" STATISTICS

A LOT OF THE TALK we hear about "the rich" and "the poor" is not really talk about people but about statistics. People in the bottom 20 percent of the income statistics are often automatically labeled "poor" and those in the top 20 percent "rich." But the human reality is often very different.

Many people who are struggling to pay the mortgage and keep a kid in college at the same time would be surprised to discover that they are included among "the rich" in the statistics. People tend to reach their peak incomes when they are middle-aged, which is also when they have their heaviest financial responsibilities.

A middle-aged father may be making twice the income of his son who has just started working, and yet not be able to spend it as freely, because the old man has to put something aside for retirement and for the rising medical expenses that aging brings, in addition to helping his children get started in life.

A divorced woman who was struggling to raise 3 children was shocked when I told her that she was among the top 5 percent of wealth-holders in the country. It was true statistically—but not very relevant from a practical point of view.

Her mortgage was almost paid off and California housing prices are outrageously high, whether for buying or renting. If she were willing to sell her home and live in a tent out in the boondocks, she would have been in great shape financially. Not really a viable alternative, but in the statistics she was included among "the rich."

Statistics about "the poor" can be just as misleading. Numbers alone do not tell you about the different circumstances that people are in. Moreover, most Americans do not stay in one income bracket for life—or even for one decade.

Small businessmen and self-employed professionals, for example, have good years and bad years, including years when they end up in the red. Are they "rich" during the good years and "poor" during the bad years? Not really—only statistically.

Millions of people graduate each June, whether from high schools, colleges, or universities. Since they have only 6 months left to work during the year they graduate, they may earn only half of what they will be making the following year, when they will be working 12 months. If half of their starting salary is low enough to put them in the bottom 20 percent this year, does that make them "poor"? Maybe not in reality, but it does on paper.

There are genuinely rich and genuinely poor people, of course. The fatal mistake is in thinking that they are the same as the people in the statistics. People who are permanently at the top or permanently at the bottom financially—the real rich and the real poor—are unlikely to add up to 10 percent of the American population. Yet political demagogues are forever talking about these two groups and justifying one policy or another in terms of stereotypes that do not apply to the vast majority of Americans.

Much income inequality is due to age. People in their forties tend to earn twice as much as people in their twenties. Disparities in wealth are even greater, since older people have been saving much longer and making mortgage payments much longer. More than half the total wealth of the country is in the hands of people over 50.

It is hardly a great social injustice when people who have been working longer have more to show for it. Those who are younger will of course become older with the passage of time and have the same economic benefits—in addition to inheriting what today's older generation leaves behind.

The political left, however, ignores these age differences and automatically treats statistical disparities in income and wealth as differences between social classes, rather than differences between age brackets. When you are in a hot political crusade, and full of moral indignation, you often don't have time to check the facts.

◆

"NEEDS"

A GROUP OF U.C.L.A. ECONOMISTS were having lunch together one day at the faculty club. One of them, named Mike, got up to go get himself some more coffee. Being a decent sort, he asked:

"Does anybody else here need coffee?"

"Need?!" another economist cried out in astonishment and outrage.

The other economists around the table also pounced on this unfortunate word, while poor Mike retreated to the coffee maker, like someone who felt lucky to escape with his life.

Partly this was good clean fun—or what passes for good clean fun among economists. But partly it was a very serious issue.

Someone is always talking about what we "need"—more child care centers, more medical research, more housing, more environmental protection. The list goes on and on. All the things we "need" would add up to far more than the Gross National Product. Obviously we cannot and will not get all the things we "need."

Why call them "needs" then? We obviously get along without them, simply because we have no choice. These "needs" are simply things we want—or that some of us want. Given that we cannot possibly have all the things we want, we have to make trade-offs. That is what economics is all about.

Words like "needs," "rights," or "entitlements," try to put some things on a pedestal, so that they don't have to face the reality of trade-offs. This is part of the higher humbug of politics.

Surely some things are really needs, you might say. If that is true, food must be one of those needs, since we would die without it. Huge agricultural surpluses are one result of this kind of mushy thinking.

There is obviously some amount of food that is urgently required to keep body and soul together. But the average American already takes in far more food than is necessary to sustain life—and in fact so much food as to make his lifespan shorter than it would be at a lower weight.

Like virtually everything else, food beyond some point ceases to be as urgently demanded and even ceases to be a benefit. When it reaches the point of being positively harmful, it can hardly be called a "need." That is why rigid words like "need" spread so much confusion in our thinking and havoc in our policies.

Prices force us into trade-offs, which is one of many reasons why the marketplace operates so much more efficiently than political allocation according to "need," "entitlement," "priorities" or other such rigid notions.

The real issue is almost never whether we should have nothing at all or some unlimited amount, or even some fixed amount of a particular good. The real issue is what kind of trade-off makes sense. That usually means having some of many things but not all we want of anything.

Prices tell us what the terms of the trade-offs are. Do we "need" more clothing? At some prices we do and at other prices we can get along with what we have. I happen to own three suits. But if clothing prices were one-tenth of what they are, I might have a wardrobe that would knock you dead.

My daughter used to make snide remarks about an old car that I drove for eight years. She stopped only when I told her that I could easily afford to get a new car, just by not paying her tuition. That's what trade-offs are all about.

If the government were giving out cars to those who "needed" them, I could have written an application that would have brought tears to your eyes. I could have gone on talk shows and worked up public sympathy over the ways my old jalopy was messing up my life—even threatening my life, because the brakes failed completely twice.

If the taxpayers were paying for it, I would have "needed" a new car. But, since it was my money that was being spent, I had a brake job instead.

Politicians take advantage of our mushy thinking by promising to meet our "need" or by giving us a "right" or "entitlement" to this or that. But let's go back to square one. Politicians don't manufacture anything except hot air. Every "need" they meet takes away from some other "need" somewhere else.

Every job the government creates is supported by resources taken out of the private sector, where those same resources could have created another job—or maybe two other jobs, given the wastefulness of government.

"Needs" are a dangerous concept. Mike the economist suffered only a momentary embarrassment from using the word. Our whole economy and society suffer much more from the mindless policies based on such misconceptions.

WHO WATCHES
THE WATCHERS?

Who watches the watchdogs?

That is the big question raised by the recent $400 million out-of-court settlement by the accounting firm of Ernst & Young, which federal agencies claimed had not done a good job of auditing some of the shaky financial institutions whose collapse is costing the taxpayers billions.

Because this was an out-of-court settlement, the validity of the charges remains unsubstantiated. Clearly, however, either the auditors or the federal agencies which audited the auditors were wrong. In short, layers upon layers of watchdogs do not guarantee effective monitoring.

The implications reach far beyond accounting, and in fact far beyond the kind of society we live in. One of the big differences between societies is in how they meet the need for monitoring.

Often the most effective monitoring is self-monitoring. That is a major part of the case for private property, for example. Both owner-operators of businesses and private homeowners typically work longer and harder on their private property than is required by any external authorities.

In the criminal law, police are only a kind of back-up system for those who are not effectively monitored by their own consciences. If the whole notion of right and wrong erodes away, as avant-garde educators seem to wish, the police cannot possibly do the whole job of keeping order. Indeed, the police themselves would have no reason to resist being corrupt.

The self-monitoring of conscience means that even people whose wrong-doing has been successfully concealed from everyone else have been known to return money they owed, to confess to unsolved crimes, and in some cases even to mete out a death penalty by committing suicide for their secret misdeeds.

Self-monitoring is reinforced by mutual monitoring among people with emotional ties to one another. Where the whole family bears the stigma of the individual member's vice, as among the Japanese, the pressures can be enormous to avoid anything that would bring disgrace upon your own flesh and blood.

Similar pressures operate in close-knit communities. Chinese business-men in various Southeast Asian countries often make deals with one another by verbal agreement, because default would mean social ruin and family disgrace. Hasidic Jews in New York are able to give one another gems to sell on consignment, without the need for legal papers, because their strong social and moral ties are more effective than legal processes would be.

The degree to which such social pressures are effective varies from one group to another and from one society to another. More honest societies can extend more credit, collect taxes more efficiently, create more joint ventures, use fewer resources for security, and enjoy higher standards of living as a result.

Such invisible, emotional, and untidy methods of constraining individual behavior and sustaining human societies have little appeal to intellectuals, who assume *a priori* that formal institutions are more effective.

All the negative features of informal controls—shame, fear, guilt, stigma—seem like arbitrary impositions to those with a rationalistic vision of man. Collective honor or shame offends their sense of individual justice.

Nothing is easier than to come up with stories—whether in literature or in real life—of someone unjustly stigmatized because of the family or group he belonged to. There is no way to dramatize equally the people who were *not* robbed, not beaten, or not killed, because of the restraining effects of the same social controls.

Because there are inevitable dilemmas in applying notions of right and wrong, increasing numbers of superficially clever people are for getting rid of both the concepts and the dilemmas they cause. A whole process called "values clarification" pervades the American public schools to do just that, to eradicate such ideas from the minds of children.

All this assumes that monitoring is either unnecesary, or that it can be carried out effectively by formal organizations. But adding layers and layers of monitors, as is necessary in Communist societies, for example, is not only costly but often less effective than the self-monitoring of people with a vested interest in their own private property.

Even in the days of Stalinist terror, more and better quality produce came out of a given amount of land in private plots than the same amount of land on collective farms. Self-monitoring by people with a vested interest in their own well-being was more effective than the whole apparatus of a totalitarian police state.

Much of the social history of the twentieth century, and especially of the last 30 years in the United States, has been a history of eroding and destroying informal systems of monitoring that worked, replacing them with more rationalistic systems that sounded good.

◆

THE NOBEL PRIZE IN ECONOMICS

FOR YEARS NOW, one of the guessing games among economists has been: When will Gary Becker get his Nobel Prize? It was almost as if there were one with his name already carved on it, and it was just a question of when those turkeys in Sweden would get around to giving it to him.

Unlike some of the more esoteric economists whose work has little applicability to the real world of the ordinary citizen, Professor Becker has applied the classic concepts of economic analysis to a whole range of common subjects not usually thought of as economic—education, crime, and racial discrimination, for example.

What Becker has done has been to explore the inner logic of these activities, showing that they are not just matters of sociological observation or psychological speculation. His first, and perhaps most important, contribution has been in his economic analysis of racial discrimination.

When Becker first began his career, no one expected economists to talk about racial issues. Single-handedly, he created a whole new field of economics. After more than three decades, Becker's analysis of racial discrimination is widely used by other economists.

Tragically, this analysis is almost totally unknown among politicians and civil rights "leaders," who often advocate policies whose counter-productive results could have been foreseen and avoided if they understood a little of what Gary Becker has been saying for decades. Given the slow rate at which the ideas of intellectual giants trickle down to the level of politicians and editorial writers, it may well be another generation before what Professor Becker published in 1957 becomes widely understood in the 21st century.

In the meantime, millions of human beings will suffer needlessly and not even understand the real sources of their suffering. Although racial discrimination has been called "an American dilemma," it is in fact widespread across vast regions of this planet, and has plagued the history of the human species for thousands of years.

Gary Becker's analysis of this phenomenon built upon the central idea that discrimination has costs, not only to the person who suffers it, but also to those who inflict it. These costs vary according to the kind of market.

There is a reason, for example, why blacks were starring in Broadway shows in the 1920s, at a time when a black woman could not get a job as a telephone operator with the phone company. The economics of the entertainment industry are very different from the economics of a public utility. Since the costs of discriminating were different in these two industries, it should not be surprising that the amount of discrimination was also different.

People did not even think about such things in this way before Gary Becker came along. Outside the economics profession, very few do even today.

One consequence is that many who wish to advance the cause of racial minorities in the United States are also pushing public policies which treat more of the American economy like public utilities, instead of like competitive industries such as entertainment.

Similar economic patterns are found in countries around the world. Apartheid in South Africa required the white minority government to treat large parts of that economy as public utilities and reduce economic competition.

For example, back during the early years of this century, the South African railroads hired far more blacks than whites, simply because the cost of discrimination would have been too high under the economic conditions that existed. Only after the South African government intervened heavily in this industry did the railroads begin to hire more whites than blacks.

In industries where the free market prevailed, apartheid laws were violated on a massive scale, as blacks were hired in larger numbers and in higher positions than the South African government's policies permitted. Hundreds of fines were imposed for such violations during a crackdown on the construction industry alone.

Wide variations in the degree of racial discrimination from one industry to another are not a result of there being people with different racial views in these different industries. These variations reflect wide differences in the cost of discriminating under different economic conditions.

In country after country, government agencies have been the biggest discriminators—whether direct discrimination or "reverse discrimination"—wherever that was politically possible. Next come private industries heavily controlled by the government, such as public utilities or government contractors.

It was no accident that laws creating racially segregated streetcars a century ago were resisted by streetcar companies across wide regions of the South, at a time when municipal transit was often both privately owned and relatively free of government control. But no such resistance to racial segregation and discrimination was put up by the public school authorities, police departments, or other government institutions in the South during the Jim Crow era.

The difference is that government agencies do not pay the costs of discrimination. Taxpayers pay those costs for them.

In winning the Nobel Prize, Gary Becker has finally received this recognition that he has so long deserved. The larger question is when his work will receive the ultimate recognition of being understood by those who discuss and make policy.

◆

HOMELESSNESS AND PROPERTY RIGHTS

ONE OF THE REASONS why the political left wins on so many issues, even when it has neither logic nor evidence on its side, is that the left knows how to package political issues. For example, "property rights versus human rights" is the way some issues are presented. Conservatives, libertarians, and other supporters of a free market economy often consider such demagoguery beneath contempt and don't bother to answer it.

That is their mistake. As long as the issue is posed as property rights versus human rights, property rights will lose every time. The tragedy is that human beings with no property worth mentioning will be big losers as well.

Homeless people sleeping out on the pavement in freezing winter weather are among the worst victims of the erosion and destruction of property rights. Among the biggest gainers are homeowners whose homes have risen in value by leaps and bounds, as zoning restrictions, rent control, and other restrictions on property rights make housing more scarce. Such restrictions have been rationalized as a way to stop "greedy developers"—a phrase often used, with a straight face, by homeowners who are profitting at a rate far beyond what any developer can hope for.

The Constitution of the United States protects property rights but judges have been very lax in enforcing these protections in recent times. Seldom will they declare zoning laws, rent control, and the like unconstitutional, even though such laws violate rights of individuals to use or sell property as they see fit. While other constitutional rights have been expanded beyond anything intended by the writers of the Constitution, property rights have been contracted.

Mobile homes have been banned from some areas. Room-renting is banned from others. Still other local authorities require that there be several acres of land around every new house that is built.

All these restrictions have one thing in common: They are designed to keep out low-income people in general and low-income minorities in particular.

Environmentalism has become part of the housing hustle. Some land has been put aside for all sorts of high-sounding reasons. On other land, you can build—but only after going through long and costly bureaucratic procedures that delay construction and drive up the price.

The environmental hustle has given a real shot in the arm to the housing restrictions game. Nowhere has environmentalism been more extreme than in California—and nowhere more successful in obstructing the building of all kinds of housing and driving its price up into the stratosphere. A prime example is Marin County, across from San Francisco.

In 1970, the average price of a house in Marin County was $33,000 but by 1980 this had shot up to $151,000. In between, Marin County created some of the most numerous, most clever and most hypocritical obstructions of housing ever seen. The era of environmental extremism has been the same era when California housing prices suddenly pulled way out in front of those in the rest of the nation and went into an orbit of their own.

Contrary to the rhetoric of the political left, property rights do not exist just to protect people fortunate enough to have property. Property rights are what make a free market economy function. If land could be sold to the highest bidder, then many a mansion would be sold and then torn down to be replaced by apartment buildings.

This is only one of the ways the poor often outbid the rich in the marketplace, because the poor are so much more numerous. But when property rights are violated and economic decisions move out of the market-place into zoning commissions, environmental agencies, and courtrooms, that is when low-income people lose leverage and are often treated as expendable.

Rather than face this plain and brutal reality, the intelligentsia in academe and the media come up with every conceivable explanation of homelessness, other than the fact that housing has been made artificially very scarce. Poverty, unemployment, and the dumping of the mentally ill on the streets have all swelled the ranks of the homeless. But all these things existed in the past without filling our streets, parks, and subway stations with homeless people.

The popular political explanations for homelessness are carefully examined—and utterly demolished—in a recently published book called *The Excluded Americans* by William Tucker. (Cato Institute, $24.95.) It is the rarest kind of book—a masterpiece written in plain English.

What Tucker finds is that it is not the cities with the worst unemployment or the fastest growing populations that have the worst homeless problem. It is the cities with the most severe restrictions on housing, including zoning and rent control, which have seen their vacancy rates shrink to the vanishing point and their communities plagued by "street people." San Francisco has had no population growth and New York and Washington have had actual population declines, but all three have unusually high rates of homelessness.

By contrast, Houston has lower rates of homelessness and higher vacancy rates in rental housing than any of these cities, even though Houston's population has grown substantially (39 percent in 15 years) and its unemployment rate has been higher than that in New York or San Francisco, and the same as that in Washington. Houston has had neither zoning nor rent control nor the environmental mania.

◆

PHOTOGRAPHY AND THE ECONOMY

PHOTOGRAPHY, like everything else, reflects both politics and economics.

Recently, in Singapore, I bought several rolls of Kodachrome film, with processing by Kodak included. You can also buy it that way in Australia, Hong Kong, Paris, and other places around the world—but not in the United States.

The U.S. government won't let Kodachrome be sold with processing included—and hasn't for more than 30 years. Inconsistently, the government has let the German color film, Agfachrome, be sold in the U.S. with processing included.

According to the bogeyman image of business that underlies American anti-trust policy, the government is supposed to be protecting us from monopoly by not allowing Kodak to sell film with this convenience. But there is no film monopoly in Singapore. Fujichrome film sat on the shelf alongside Kodachrome, and I bought some of both.

All around the world, Kodak faces competition from Japanese film made by Fuji, German film made by Agfa, and British film made by Ilford. Competition is what really protects the consumer, not ridiculous anti-trust policies. In addition, competition forces all these film manufacturers to keep improving their products, under threat of losing millions of dollars if a competitor nudges ahead of them with a better product.

Where there is no competition, progress is slow or non-existent. In the Soviet Union, for example, a 1936-model German camera has been produced and sold, on into the 1980s. The dies used to make this camera were captured when Soviet troops went into Germany during world War II. These dies were then sent to the U.S.S.R., where this camera has since been manufactured under a Soviet brand name.

The camera is still not as well made as it was in Germany more than half a century ago. Naturally, no one in the outside world wants it. But Soviet consumers have little choice.

Meanwhile, out in the competitive world market, cameras are being improved by leaps and bounds. The new camera will do everything but take the film to the store to be developed.

But our own deep thinkers find it hard to get the picture—not only as regards the photographic industry, but business in general. Any company that makes a superior product is likely to attract vast numbers of consumers. When that happens, deep thinkers speak of it as one company "controlling" a large "share" of the market.

Usually, the company doesn't "control" anything. The minute somebody else makes a better product, that large percentage share can vanish into thin air.

Thirty years ago, the Graflex Corporation made a big, boxy camera with a bellows. It was called the Speed Graphic, and almost every press photographer in the country used one. In the language of the deep thinkers, the Graflex Corporation "controlled" almost the entire market for press cameras.

Today, the camera and the company that made it are both long gone. After decades of pre-eminence, they were wiped out completely in a few years, when changes in technology made it possible for press photographers to get good pictures with smaller 35mm cameras.

Market control is even more illusory today, when the market for many products is international. No matter how big an American company becomes, American consumers usually have plenty of choices of buying the same product from somebody else, located here or overseas. Neither Kodak nor General Motors can control the market.

Talk about "controlling" the market is usually bogeyman talk, but it is taken in deadly seriousness by many "experts" in anti-trust policy. The harassment of American companies under these policies does nothing to benefit the consumer. It only makes it harder for American businesses to compete with foreign businesses that don't have this nonsense to contend with.

—————————————————————— ◆ ——————————————————————

SOCIAL SECURITY FRAUD

IF YOU WATCHED THE ASTRONAUTS in space or the American troops in
Panama, you were seeing your Social Security dollars at work.

The image of Social Security is that it is a fund into which "contributions"
are made and accumulated, to be paid out later as retirement pensions. The
reality is that the money is spent as fast as it comes in.

Social Security money is spent for whatever other government money is
spent for—to renovate the White House, build nuclear missiles, or give
Congressmen a pay raise. It is just another tax collected from the public. But
instead of being called a tax, it is called F.I.C.A. (Federal Insurance Contrib-
utor's Act).

Not only is Social Security a political fraud. It also helps politicians create
another fraud by concealing part of the national debt.

It goes like this: When money comes in as Social Security contributions,
and is spent immediately, like other taxes, the government issues its bonds
as I.O.U.s to the Social Security Administration for the money it took. The
national debt consists of government bonds but bonds held by government
agencies are not counted, on grounds that the government cannot be in debt
to itself. Therefore the national debt is lower—on paper.

In reality, the government owes money to all those people who have
been promised pensions in exchange for their Social Security taxes. That
debt just doesn't go on the books as part of the national debt.

Social Security has never been an insurance system, though that is the
Big Lie used to sell it to the public politically. An insurance company has to
have enough assets accumulated to cover all the benefits it has to pay out.
Social Security has never had that.

Social Security operates like a chain letter or a pyramid club. Those who
pay in early get money from those who pay in later. This was a great game
politically when there was a large "baby boom" generation working and paying
Social Security taxes to cover the pensions of the smaller generation that
went before them.

It won't be nearly as much fun when the baby-boomers retire and have
to be supported by the smaller generation coming after them. Chain letters
and pyramid clubs are illegal for a reason. Somebody has to get left holding
the bag when new membership stops expanding.

That is Social Security's basic problem. Like chain letters and pyramid clubs, Social Security paid off well for those who got in first and received back far more money than they paid in. But when the baby-boomers retire in the 21st century, the government is either going to have to welch on its promises to them or jack up the Social Security tax on those who are working.

There are all sorts of ways of welching. Doing so directly would be bad politics but the government can pay off with inflated dollars, tax part of the benefits away with one hand while handing them out with the other, or just raise the retirement age.

The liberals' reply to complaints about all the book-keeping sleight-of-hand that goes on with Social Security is: Why worry? The government will always pay off on Social Security, one way or another. Senator Daniel Patrick Moynihan said: "Social Security payments have never been a day late or a dollar short."

Just a few short years ago, Lincoln Savings & Loan could have made the same statement. No matter how financially unsound any institution is, it is not bankrupt until it is bankrupt, to paraphrase Yogi Berra. Politicians will undoubtedly patch things up as they go along. But patches are not free.

Once we understand that Social Security is essentially a way of collecting more taxes without calling them taxes, we can see that Senator Moynihan's recent proposal to reduce Social Security "contributions" is just another tax cut—at a time when Congress is pretending to be trying to reduce the deficit. Sometimes a cut in tax *rates* can generate more tax *revenue* by stimulating more economic activity. No one has ever claimed such a thing for the Moynihan plan.

All that a Social Security tax cut would accomplish would be to increase the deficit and enable the big spenders to say that we need to raise some other tax to deal with it. Congress is full of tax junkies. They have gone for more than a year now without a fix, and it's obviously giving them withdrawal symptoms.

◆

PROFIT WITHOUT HONOR

IN ANCIENT TIMES, it was said that a prophet was without honor in his own home. Today, a profit is without honor in the media and academia.

Nothing is more common than seeing a TV reporter describing the misdeeds of some businessman and concluding indignantly: "Human beings were sacrificed for the sake of profit." Variations on this theme are pervasive at our leading colleges and universities.

Intellectuals have a gift for seizing on the incidental and missing the essential. Blaming profit is like saying that what was wrong with Nazi Germany was that certain dreaded German words led to millions of human beings being sent to concentration camps.

If the orders had been in Chinese or in Spanish, the results would have been just as horrible. There is no point crusading against the German language.

The crusade against profit is just as irrational. What is really wrong is that human beings put their own selfish interests ahead of the well-being of their fellow man. They have been doing this for thousands of years, long before anybody ever thought of capitalism or of profit.

In a primitive society based on cattle, some people will sacrifice the well-being—or the lives—of others, in order to have a bigger herd. In modern dictatorships, some people sacrifice the lives of millions, in order to have power. In a society based on capitalism, the same selfishness takes the form of preoccupation with money—whether that money is called profit, salary, or government grants.

You could abolish money tomorrow without making a dent in the problem. All you would do is add a multitude of new problems, as the economy went haywire without a payment system.

Some of the greatest tragedies of the twentieth century have come from attempts to change "the system" so that the particular form which human selfishness took in that particular system would no longer exist. Fanatical efforts and enormous suffering went into destroying the czarist regime in Russia and establishing the Communist regime.

You no longer had hereditary despots or "the evils of capitalism" in Russia. But the new despots outdid the old, whether in tyranny, terror, or slaughter. Both in the political system and in the economic system, the evils of man were simply expressed in a different format, without being lessened in any way. On the contrary, the greater power of the state made these evils more deadly.

The Soviet experience was by no means unique. The French Revolution of 1789 destroyed the old royalty and nobility, only to create new and bloodier tyrants inside a decade. When Napoleon took over from the revolutionaries, his military adventures led to Frenchmen being slaughtered all over Europe, in pursuit of Napoleon's vision of glory.

The past generation has seen variations on this theme all over the world. The autocratic rule of Emperor Haile Selassie in Ethiopia now seems like the good old days, compared to the genocidal ruthlessness of his Marxist successors. In some Third World countries like Uganda and Cambodia, the departure of Western colonialists only set the stage for horrors differing only in scale from those of Hitler and the Nazis.

Nothing is easier than attacking a system. All systems—political, economic, or moral—cramp people's style and they don't like it. Nothing is more certain than the abuse of power by those who have it, under any and all systems, so there will always be legitimate grievances.

The fatal step is to go from grievances to the destruction of the system under which they occur. Radical critics—especially young ones—are quick to take that step. I must include myself, since I was a young Marxist. Many things looked bad to me, so I thought the whole system should be changed from top to bottom.

What forced me to change my mind was discovering over the years that things were even worse than I thought. People did awful things, not just here but all around the world, not just now but across thousands of years of history.

It was enough to turn your stomach—and make you realize that re-shuffling politicians and re-naming institutions was not going to do the job, even if you called it a revolution. History was especially disillusioning. It showed that some of my pet ideas had already been tried, and had blown up in people's faces.

Not all historic changes have been for the worse. But the most successful changes have been those that started out recognizing that man himself is the problem—and establishing human institutions to keep any given set of people from having too much power, no matter how noble or glorious their rhetoric might sound.

Anyone who has read *The Federalist Papers* knows that those who wrote the American Constitution had very big doubts about human beings in general and especially about trusting anybody with unbridled power. That skepticism shows in the Constitution they wrote and was a big part of its success over a period of two centuries, while more ambitious political experiments came and went, or turned cancerous and stayed.

The economic counterpart of Constitutional checks and balances is an economy where everyone who wants profits—or wages, or money in any other form—has to compete with everybody else. Its results aren't perfect, by any means, but it beats the next best thing by a big margin.

◆

"NON-PROFIT"
WITHOUT HONOR

ONE OF THE REASONS we have so many counterproductive policies is that we cannot discuss their specifics without getting hypnotized by words.

Among those hypnotic words, nothing brings thinking to a halt quicker than the label "non-profit." Money is money, no matter what it is called. But everything from public attitudes to federal laws are different if you call an organization "non-profit."

There are 10 universities which each take in more than a billion dollars a year in revenue and 16 whose assets exceed a billion dollars, led by Harvard with $6.5 billion in assets. But because that money is under a non-profit halo, it escapes taxation. How are these organizations different from other organizations?

Do the people who run non-profit organizations donate their time, like Red Cross volunteers? Don't you believe it.

Presidents of every major private university in this country receive six-figure salaries. The salaries of college athletic coaches often exceed the salaries of their college president—and sometimes exceed the salary of the governor of the state or the President of the United States. Several college athletic coaches take home more than half a million dollars a year—all in "amateur" sports at non-profit institutions.

Six-figure salaries are also not uncommon in so-called "public television," another non-profit organization. The MacNeil-Lehrer news hour is a fine program, but do not believe for a moment that MacNeil and Lehrer are out working in a factory somewhere during the day and donate their time in the evening to broadcast the news.

The issue is not whether these people deserve the pay they receive. The issue is whether there is any fundamental difference between them and others whose money comes from organizations whose earnings are called by the dreaded word "profit." Many a small businessman would be happy to receive as profit, in a good year, the incomes that many individuals are guaranteed every year as salary in non-profit organizations.

Many non-profit organizations in fact conduct business in competition with ordinary firms that have to pay taxes and meet other requirements, from which non-profit organizations are exempt. All sorts of products and services are marketed by non-profit organizations in competition with similar commercial products and services. Ocean Spray cranberry juice, Land O'Lakes butter, Sunkist oranges, *Nation's Business* Magazine, various electricity-generating companies and credit unions, are just some examples.

A level playing field for competition is not just a matter of fairness to competitors. It's a matter of fairness to the public, whose whole standard of living depends on the efficiency of the economy.

Efficiency requires that resources be used by whoever can turn inputs into outputs at the lowest cost. If tax laws and other laws apply differently to competing organizations, then the survivors in this competition will not be those who can produce the most bang for the buck, but those who can keep their bucks from being taxed.

Where any organization is both tax-exempt and is supported by donations from people who cannot possibly monitor its many internal operations, then there is virtually no limit to its waste and inefficiency. Colleges and universities are a classic example.

Professors make most of the decisions in leading colleges and universities, but they know little and care less about the financial condition of their institutions. Colleges spend their money until it runs out—and then either raise tuition or turn to the government for help, or both.

When Bowdoin College got into financial trouble last year, its professors first learned about it by reading the story in a local newspaper. One of the college's own administrators admitted that they had simply gotten into the habit of financing whatever new projects sounded good—and eventually this caught up with them.

Corporations who operate that way find their creditors breathing down their necks and face the threat of a takeover by others who think they can run the business better. The threat alone can be enough to make them shape up.

Protecting non-profit organizations from having to compete on a level playing field insulates waste and makes the whole economy less efficient. The lofty hypocrisy of many non-profits only adds insult to injury.

———————————————   ◆   ———————————————

GEORGE J. STIGLER
(1911–1991)

THE OBITUARIES IDENTIFY PROFESSOR GEORGE J. STIGLER of the University of Chicago as a Nobel Prize–winning economist, but that was not the half of it.

In a world of self-promoting academics, coining buzzwords and aligning themselves on the side of the angels of the moment, George Stigler epitomized a rare integrity as well as a rare intellect. He jumped on no bandwagons, beat no drums for causes, created no personal cult.

He did the work of a scholar and a teacher—both superbly—and found that sufficient. If you wanted to learn, and above all if you wanted to learn how to think—how to avoid the vague words, fuzzy thoughts, or maudlin sentiments that cloud over reality—then Stigler was your man.

Those of us privileged to have known Stigler as his students or his colleagues will never forget his quick and sharp wit—and those rash enough to cross swords with him in controversy have the scars to show for it.

His wit was the wit of distilled wisdom, not mere cleverness with words. When he said "widely accepted facts are often wrong," he was saying something that becomes more painfully clear the more research you do.

Of other Nobel Prize winners who make many grandiloquent statements on things they know nothing about, Stigler said that they "issue stern ultimata to the public on almost a monthly basis, and sometimes on no other basis."

In reviewing an economics book written in a rambling, convoluted style, Stigler wrote the first paragraph of his review in the same style. Then he began the second paragraph: "If the reader can wade through 508 pages of this style of writing . . ."

Professor Frank Knight, one of Stigler's mentors at the University of Chicago, was a man "who would not have hesitated to tell Gabriel that his horn needed tuning," Stigler said. The University of Chicago economics department has had many men like that, including George Stigler.

Once, after leaving a committee meeting, Stigler said: "I don't know why people think it was such a feat for Lindbergh to fly across the Atlantic alone. If he could have flown across the Atlantic with a committee, now that would have been a feat."

Stigler's classroom was an intellectual Demolition Derby where fashionable cant and tempting fallacies were sent crashing and ended up on the junk heap, where they belonged. He never seemed troubled by the popular question: "But what would you put in its place?" Stigler was not a social engineer, but a thinker who was teaching others to think.

For Stigler, economics was not some magic formula to be used to produce personal fortune or national miracles. Economics was for him a body of knowledge "that prevents hopeless but costly endeavors." He was not looking for "solutions," but was exposing the dangerous illusion that politicians can pull rabbits out of a hat to give us free lunches.

If teaching us how to analyze and warning us against free lunches seems like a somewhat limited role for economics, it was in keeping with Stigler's view of "our disgraceful ignorance of the effects of past policies" and his conviction that "only a tiny set of policies have been studied with even moderate care."

The era spanned by Stigler's life included two decades—the 1930s and the 1960s—marked by passionate delusions, in economics as elsewhere. He specialized in two areas where those delusions were especially prevalent, industrial organization and the history of economics, so his skepticism was especially needed.

"Monopoly has become as popular a subject in economics as sin has been in religion," Stigler said. The analogy was apt, for much that has been said about monopoly by economists specializing in industrial organization has been evangelical in its fervor, rather than logical in its reasoning—and demands for evidence have sometimes been considered as shocking as heresy.

Among those studying the history of economic theories, it was once fashionable to say that great events provoke great intellectual breakthroughs in economics. Stigler refused to go along with this romantic notion.

"A war may devastate a continent and yet raise no new theoretical questions," he said.

He never said much (if anything) about the sacred duty of a scholar to seek the truth rather than notoriety. He simply lived it. That was an old-fashioned virtue that deserves an old-fashioned word: Noble. That's more important than Nobel.

◆

PART IV
THE POLITICAL SCENE

THE CENTURY OF
THE INTELLECTUAL

THE TWENTIETH CENTURY has been the century of the intellectual—and nowhere more so than in politics.

The two leading totalitarian regimes of this century, Nazi Germany and the Soviet Union, were created by writers and talkers: Adolf Hitler and V. I. Lenin. Hitler's *Mein Kampf,* and Lenin's *Imperialism* and other writings, were what put them on the map. The quality of their writings, in terms of logic or evidence, may have been shabby beyond belief. But these were masterpieces of propaganda.

Lenin's tracts rescued Marxism from the utter failures of its predictions and provided a whole new world vision, in which his political enemies were cast as international arch-villains, and Lenin's own followers as heroic agents of destiny.

Marxist-Leninist tracts like *Imperialism* gave comprehensive, dramatic and bitter explanations of the world's ills and discontents. Any sophomore could find in them the master keys to history, without the drudgery of having to know the facts or cope with the complexities of reality.

Hitler likewise created his own universe of the mind, peopled by whole races assigned their disparate roles in the grand scheme of history, and made titans or devils according to one man's imagination. Drivel? Yes. Powerfully effective? Also yes.

Some might say that these were pseudo-intellectuals or even anti-intellectuals, in terms of the quality of their reasoning or their use of evidence. But being an intellectual is an occupation, and the quality of their work does not change their occupation. A bad surgeon is still a surgeon—a deadly menace to the unsuspecting, but a surgeon nonetheless.

Being intellectuals was not an incidental part of the political careers of twentieth century dictators like Lenin, Hitler, or Mao. Their writings and sayings were the key instruments of their rise to power, just as military prowess was the key to Napoleon's. Moreover, their appeal was not just to the gullible masses, but to other intellectuals, including scholars, literary giants, and others with impeccable credentials in the world of ideas.

If totalitarianism was the ugly beast of twentieth century politics, its beauty was admired by the likes of George Bernard Shaw and Thorstein

Veblen, and its apologists ranged from Pulitzer Prize–winning journalist Walter Duranty of the *New York Times* to whole armies of fellow-travelers in the media and academic world of their time.

The pilgrimages of intellectuals to the lands of the dictators— to Stalinist Russia, Maoist China, or Castro's Cuba—have been among the amazing stories of this century, as eminent scholars and literary figures have come back to gush over the "progress" of tyrannies whose own people were making desperate escapes whenever they could.

In short, totalitarianism has been an intellectual phenomenon. It appealed to the same susceptibilities of intellectuals as other crusades that have seized the imagination of the educated and the articulate—so-called "thinking people"—such as the eugenics movement in the early part of the century and environmentalism in the later decades.

What all these movements have in common is a sense of a revelation grasped only by the anointed, but a revelation that needs to be imposed on the benighted masses for their own good. Could anything be more of an ego trip, or more in keeping with intellectuals' exalted view of themselves, or their resentment at seeing wealth and power in the hands of lesser beings?

Nothing as mundane as mere evidence can be allowed to threaten a vision so deeply satisfying. People who escaped from totalitarian paradises, and who told tales of the horrors there, were dismissed as political enemies spreading lies.

Where the facts were too blatant to deny, the explanation was that these were "growing pains" of a new society or "local excesses," and we were reminded that "you can't make an omelette without breaking eggs." The fatal talent of the intelligentsia is facility with words—and a blindness to the fact that reality is not nearly so malleable as language.

Only after the official archives were opened in the last days of the Soviet Union did the unthinkable horrors of an evil empire become undeniable. Yes, there was a deliberately engineered famine in the Ukraine under Stalin— and its victims exceeded even the horrifying estimates in Robert Conquest's classic study of the subject. Yes, the Soviets carried out a mass murder of Polish military officers and—we learned more recently—the execution of American prisoners from as far back as World War II, when we were supposedly "allies."

The past is irrevocable, but many of the factors behind its tragedies are still at work in the present, and are a danger to the future. The issues change— eugenics is not environmentalism—but the dogmatism and the ego behind the dogmatism are the same.

◆

MEDIA BIAS

OVER THE YEARS, studies have repeatedly shown people in the mass media
to be overwhelmingly of the political left. However, that kind of media bias
may not be as important as a bias inherent in the way the media operate,
irrespective of the opinions of the people involved.

Radio, television, and motion pictures can readily dramatize an individual situation, in a way in which the larger relationships behind that situation
cannot be dramatized.

For example, the media cannot identify, much less dramatize, all those
individuals who would have come down with some deadly disease, if it were
not for their being vaccinated. But nothing is easier to dramatize than the
rare individual who caught the disease from the vaccine and is now devastated
by illness, crippled, or dying.

When the government creates some new program, nothing is easier than
to show whatever benefits that program produces. Indeed, those who run
the program will be more than cooperative in bringing those benefits to the
attention of the media. But it is virtually impossible to trace the taxes that
paid for the program back to their sources and to show the alternative uses
of that same money that could have been far more beneficial.

In short, the built-in bias of the media is to show what happens right
under our noses, with little or no regard to what that has cost elsewhere.

A California farmer can always show the television audience the abundant
crop he has been able to grow because of federal water projects. But no one
can videotape the crops that would have been grown elsewhere, at less cost
to the economy, if there were no federal subsidies to encourage the wasting
of water in the California desert.

There is likewise no way the television camera can show which unemployed people would have had jobs, if the minimum wage laws had not made
them too expensive to hire at their current levels of skill and experience—
and thereby cut them off from acquiring the additional skills and experience
they need.

There is no way to identify and interview those people who would be
living comfortably in New York City buildings that are currently abandoned
and boarded-up because rent control laws have made them economically
unviable.

Regardless of the ideological bias of people in the media, there is no way for the camera to show all the businesses that would exist in the absence of government red tape and mandated costs.

Deceptive appearances have been with us long before the rise of the modern mass media. But never before have those appearances been able to reach so many people, with so much immediacy and so much seeming reality.

What makes the built-in bias of the mass media so dangerous is that it adds leverage to a similar bias in political decision-making toward doing good right under our noses, without regard to wider and longer-run implications.

Could slavery have been ended by the Civil War if television news had shown daily scenes of the horrors of Sherman's march through Georgia, or the appalling sufferings of civilians in besieged Vicksburg? The televised sufferings of the war in Indo-China helped bring it to an end—leading to even more suffering and even more deaths after the Communists took over that region, but these sufferings (including the killing fields of Kampuchea) were not televised.

Not being able to televise the horrors under totalitarian regimes is another built-in bias of the media, which can only show suffering in a free society—thereby making such societies easier to undermine.

The media can even build up sympathy for murderers by interviewing their mothers or wives, who proclaim their innocence, or fellow criminals who give them an alibi by saying that they were somewhere else when the crime was committed. Just the sight of a forlorn man on death row can be touching.

The media cannot show that same man exulting in the savagery of the crime which brought him there, cannot show his sadistic joy when he was raping and torturing a little girl tearfully pleading for her life. If they could show that on television, many of those people who gather outside prison to protest his execution would instead be inside volunteering to pull the switch.

The dangerous dramatizing of half-truths is the fatal talent of the television or movie camera. Even with honest and balanced people, that danger would be ever present, and would need to be constantly guarded against. With a media overwhelmingly of one ideological bent, human bias and media bias only reinforce one another.

NBC News' notorious rigged "test" of a truck that burst into flames on impact is only further proof that the motto "pictures don't lie" is itself dangerously misleading.

◆

WARS OVER VALUES

CULTURAL WARS ARE DIRTY WARS, much like guerilla warfare in the jungles, with no regard for the rules of the Geneva Convention.

Warfare over traditional values versus avante-garde values is raging all across the United States today, from the art galleries to the armed forces, and from the kindergarten to the Supreme Court. At issue is whose cultural values shall prevail and who shall make the decisions that reflect those values.

The categorical language of "rights" is widely used as a weapon in these cultural wars. Those who are pushing a woman's "right" to go into military combat, for example, are in effect saying that the decisions of the military commanders responsible for the lives of thousands of troops, and the decisions of the American society as to the social roles of the sexes, are all to be superseded by the visions of self-anointed and politically organized feminist advocacy groups.

The particulars of the arguments—the physical strength of the sexes, the performance of women in the military, etc.—are in one sense all beside the point. The question is not what to decide, but *who is to decide*. As elsewhere in the cultural wars, the issue is whether a vocal elite should get the power to pre-empt the decisions of others.

To the anointed, the use of words like "rights" is sufficient to put one coterie's opinions above discussion and the word "stereotypes" is enough to put the values of the society at large beneath discussion. They don't want discussion, they want power.

One of the more remarkable "rights" to emerge in recent years is the right to the taxpayers' money for anything that chooses to call itself "art"—regardless of whether the taxpayers or voters like what is produced, and regardless of whether the clear intent of this "art" is in fact to insult the values and beliefs of the public.

For people to decide what their own money is to be spent for is "censorship" in the Newspeak of the anointed.

More generally, the cultural wars are being waged to get decision-making powers transferred to elites who do not pay, either in money or in other ways. Family responsibilities, for example, have been taken over by schools, courts, social agencies, and others who pay no price if their decisions turn out disastrously for children or their parents, or for the whole society.

The basic thrust of the so-called "consumer movement" is likewise a drive for pre-empting the consumer's choice, not simply informing it. The "consumer must be protected at times from his own indiscretion and vanity," Ralph Nader said in his first article, published in *The Nation* in 1959.

It is much the same story in the economic sphere, where having an economic "plan," or perhaps even an "industrial policy" or an "energy policy" are all widely and uncritically regarded among opinion elites as good things in themselves. But government "planning" is not an alternative to chaos. It is a pre-emption of other people's plans.

Whether the sphere of activity is art, military combat, law, schools, or the economy, the issue is whether elite pre-emption shall replace both individual autonomy and democratic choice.

The courts are a major battleground in these wars over cultural values, for they are well-positioned to pre-empt the decisions of others by "interpreting" the Constitution to ban or promote whatever the judges want banned or promoted.

The bitter struggles over Supreme Court nominees in recent years have reflected this key role of the courts in imposing policies so repugnant to the public that elected representatives would not dare vote them into law.

Criminals' judge-created "rights," busing, affirmative action, and abortion, are just some of the policies pre-empted from the democratic process by judicial fiat. The issue, as Judge Robert H. Bork has said, is whether "intellectual class values" shall "continue to be enacted into law by the Supreme Court." The concern expressed by Justices O'Connor, Kennedy, and Souter as to how their ruling in the recent case of *Planned Parenthood vs. Casey* would be seen by "the thoughtful part of the Nation" suggests that elite pre-emption is still in favor, even among Justices labelled "conservative."

The pre-emptive class is undoubtedly sincere. People are never more sincere than when they assume their own superiority. Nor are they ever more ruthless. J. A. Schumpeter said that the first thing a man will do for his ideals is lie.

Disingenuous words, twisted statistics, and misleading labels are all part of the dirty war over cultural values. Cultural wars are so desperate because they are not simply about the merits or demerits of particular policies. They are about the anointed's whole conception of themselves—about whether they are in the heady role of a vanguard or in the pathetic role of pretentious and silly people, infatuated with themselves.

◆

THE LEFT VERSUS
THE COMMON MAN

ONE OF THE BITTERSWEET THINGS about growing old is realizing how mistaken you were when you were young. As a young political leftist, I saw the left as the voice of the common man. Nothing could be further from the truth.

The rhetoric of the political left often invokes the name of the common man, but their interest in ordinary people is at best like the ASPCA's interest in dogs and cats. No one at the ASPCA has ever suggested putting cats and dogs on their board of directors.

Running left-wing movements has always been the prerogative of spoiled rich kids. This pattern goes all the way back to the days when an over-indulged and affluent young man named Karl Marx combined with another over-indulged youth from a wealthy family named Friedrich Engels to create the Communist ideology.

The phoniness of the claim to be a movement of the working class was blatant from the beginning. When Engels was elected as a delegate to the Communist League in 1847, in his own words, "a working man was proposed for appearances sake, but those who proposed him voted for me." It may have been the first rigged "election" of the Communist movement but it was certainly not the last.

The original Fabian socialists in Britain were at least candid that theirs was not a working class movement. George Bernard Shaw, a leading Fabian, spoke of the working class as "detestable." When they died, he said, "there is no need on earth why they should be replaced by people like themselves." The anointed have always wanted to create their own kind of people, as well as their own kind of society.

While the ASPCA focuses its efforts on the well-being of cats and dogs, the political left focuses its efforts on getting power. Ordinary people are to be used as means to that end—and as guinea pigs for social experiments.

In country after country, labor unions who helped the Communists to power have discovered too late that they have far fewer rights under communism than under capitalism. Going on strike can land you in prison, as the leaders of Solidarity in Poland can tell you.

Peasants have also been taken in by the glowing rhetoric of the left in a number of countries. The magic phrase "land reform" has gained the support of many peasants who aspired to be free and independent farmers with their own little piece of land. No sooner have Marxist regimes consolidated their power than the peasants discover too late that they are now working for the state, which tells them what to grow, when to grow it, and how much (actually, how little) they will be paid for it.

This game has been played, again and again, around the world. But its rhetoric remains as seductive as ever, not only to illiterate masses in Third World countries but especially to intellectuals in the industrialized Western nations.

The fascination of intellectuals with words often blinds them to realities. The fact that others have the same rhetoric has repeatedly led intellectuals to the fallacy that they are pursuing the same goals. That is why Communists so often find intellectuals to be "useful idiots."

The latest twist in this story is now taking place in South Africa. Apartheid is so disgusting to most decent people in the West that it never occurs to them that apartheid is a political gold mine to a Marxist-Leninist seeking power—and there are no other kinds of Marxist-Leninists.

The Soviet-backed and Soviet-armed African National Congress, with Communists prominent among its leadership, has been able to get the support of all sorts of non-Communist intellectuals (including clergymen), merely by using all the right rhetoric about "one man, one vote" and the like.

Why would the Soviet Union be spending hard cash to get blacks in South Africa democratic rights that their own people don't have? If mineral-rich South Africa fell into the Soviet orbit, it would give the Communist bloc a near-monopoly of many of the strategic minerals on this planet. But "useful idiots" in the West don't even discuss that fateful possibility.

Back in the 1920s, the political left in South Africa was pushing for more discrimination against blacks, not less. Marxists around the world used a variation on a slogan from the *Communist Manifesto*: "Workers of the World Unite and Fight for a White South Africa."

Why the difference, compared to today? There is no difference. In both eras, the Marxists said whatever was calculated to bring them closer to power. They leave the illusions to others.

---◆---

SUPER SAFETY

POLITICS AND ECONOMICS are not just different. They are antagonistic.

The basic premise of economics is scarcity: There is never enough to satisfy everybody. That means there is no free lunch, no "solutions" but only trade-offs.

Politics is full of "solutions." There are free lunches for every voting bloc. The name of the game in politics is to do a little good, right under your nose, and ignore all the harm created elsewhere.

The clash of these two approaches came out recently over the issue of safety seats for babies in airplanes. Someone discovered that some infants who died in plane crashes might have survived if they had been strapped into their own special seats instead of being held in a parent's arms.

The political answer was a law requiring infants and small children to have their own seats—which is to say, requiring parents to pay for an extra seat.

It doesn't matter politically that very few planes crash, that very few infants are killed, or that not all of them would be saved by having their own seats. The political answer is: If only one life is saved, that is worth whatever it costs.

Not everybody has enough money to be able to afford to ignore costs. Some people are going to give up on taking a plane and drive instead. Since cars have far higher fatality rates per passenger mile than airplanes, more lives are likely to be lost from this political "solution."

Safety issues often bring on political "solutions." It is so easy and so tempting to say something lofty and pious like: "A human life is worth more than any amount of money."

Lots of people talk that way but nobody acts that way. If you could get a million dollars by flying a thousand miles, chances are you would do it—even though this would increase the dangers to your life. But you wouldn't do it if your life were literally of infinite value.

Despite all the hysteria of the super-safety freaks, the lifespan of Americans keeps increasing. How can that be, when everything is supposed to be toxic, cancer-causing, or unsafe in a thousand other ways? One reason is that wealth does more to extend human life than many of the safety crusades that create so much political noise.

Prosperous countries, like prosperous people, generally live longer. If we buy the political rhetoric about how safety is more important than economics, it could cost more lives than it saves. The people who talk that way often already have theirs.

It's a different ball game for those whose incomes won't let them live in the healthiest places, eat the best food or get the best medical care. In the Third World, more prosperity can save more lives than all the safety rules anybody can dream up.

Unfortunately, a growing number of people are overdosing on moral one-upmanship. They get their jollies denouncing "unsafe" things. Since all things are unsafe to one degree or another, they have an inexhaustible source for moral exhibitionism.

The question is not why some people carry on like this. The question is why the rest of us take them seriously. We need to realize that there are only trade-offs, not "solutions."

When some life-saving medicine is kept off the market because it's not perfectly safe, we need to ask how many lives are being lost in the name of safety and how many would be lost if the medicine were used. Many lives are being saved in Europe by medicines which cannot be sold in the United States because they are not yet safe enough.

When a pesticide is banned because its residues in the soil are unsafe, we need to ask how many more people will die from malaria and other insect-borne diseases. In just one small country, Sri Lanka, the number of malaria cases went up by a quarter of a million people after DDT was banned. We can't afford that kind of "safety."

——————————————————— ◆ ———————————————————

THE TIME OF THE TINKERERS

MANY YEARS AGO, the legendary manager of the New York Giants, John J. McGraw, found himself with a teenage ballplayer on his team, a boy with a great natural ability to hit, but with a completely unorthodox batting style: He lifted his front foot in the air before hitting the ball.

Since this lad—his name was Mel Ott—had no professional experience, the usual thing would have been to send him down to the minor leagues to get some seasoning and then bring him back after he had proven himself. But McGraw was not willing to risk that.

He knew that most managers would not be able to resist trying to change that odd batting style—and he also knew that tinkering with it might upset the boy's natural swing and destroy a real talent. He kept young Ott on the bench with the Giants, sending him into games here and there, in situations where his inexperience was unlikely to hurt the team.

The rest, as they say, was history. Mel Ott went on to become one of the great sluggers of all time, a star right-fielder, and ultimately a member of the Baseball Hall of Fame. And he always lifted his right foot in the air before hitting the ball.

What John J. McGraw understood is what far too many intellectuals and politicians have never understood—that you cannot simply tinker with something that works. Yet few maxims are harder to follow than the simple admonition: "If it ain't broke, don't fix it."

Fixing it is what many politicians, intellectuals and—increasingly—judges are all about. It is also becoming clear that President Clinton's promise to fix the economy is going to be carried out, even though the economic recovery that is already underway shows that it is not broke.

Implicit in the activist conception of government is the assumption that you can take the good things in a complex system for granted, and just improve the things that are not so good. What is lacking in this conception is any sense that a society, an institution, or even a single human being, is an intricate system of fragile inter-relationships, whose complexities are little understood and easily destabilized.

You cannot simply accept the benefits of a complex market economy and then decide that you will improve it by tacking on automobile mileage requirements here, special requirements for the disabled there, more reg-ulatory red tape somewhere else, etc., and not expect it all to affect the whole system.

You cannot turn public school systems across the nation into cultural battlegrounds over homosexuality, animal rights, racial issues, environmen-talism, and innumerable other ideological controversies, without expecting that academic subjects will suffer from the time and distraction invested in these other things.

The temptation to do good on some particular issue right under their noses is especially strong among those who do not have to pay the conse-quences. Intellectuals, politicians, and judges are especially susceptible to this temptation.

Too many judicial activist decisions are both conceived and criticized in terms of how they affect the particular case or the particular class of people involved in that case. The broader question is: How does it affect the whole legal system, and the whole society, when decision-makers everywhere are deprived of a predictable set of ground rules—the very reason for law—and must hedge and hesitate for fear of what some judge's notion of "evolving standards" might turn out to be?

Much of the history of the past 30 years has been a history of tinkering with isolated problems, with no sense of how that affects the rest of the system.

Many of those who have, for decades, supported an orgy of destruction of low-income housing all across the country, under high-sounding names like "urban renewal," or who have prevented new apartment buildings from being built because of "environmental" concerns, are today among those most shocked by "homelessness." Many of those who have been undermining law enforcement for decades are likewise among the most shocked at the growth of violent crime.

None of this means that reforms should never take place. Even such a classic conservative thinker as Edmund Burke said: "A society without the means of change is without the means of its conservation."

We must attend to the defects of the state, Burke said, in the same spirit as we would attend to the wounds of our father. It is a sobering responsibility, not an "exciting" opportunity to experiment.

Above all, we must not take things apart that we do not know how to put back together. Yet that is what schools are doing when they tinker with the moral beliefs that children were taught at home through "values clarification" programs in the classrooms.

Few of those with "Congressman" or "Justice" in front of their name, or with Ph.D. after it, seem to understand what John J. McGraw understood decades ago.

---------------------------------- ◆ ----------------------------------

NIBBLING AWAY FREEDOM

SOMETIMES SMALL THINGS tell you about big things. The tempest in a teapot over the colorization of movies, or over whether men's clubs should be forced to admit women, shows a mindset that is not merely petty but dangerous.

A new process turns old black and white movies into color movies—usually with miserable-looking colors. Congress has held hearings on this.

All sorts of Hollywood big names have testified, urging Congress to pass laws forbidding colorization.

The idea is that some of these old movies are "classics" which are being "ruined." The reality, however, is that the original movies are untouched. Copies of the movies are made and then colorized, just as you can buy a copy of the Mona Lisa and draw a mustache on it.

If people don't like the way the colorized copies look, they don't have to watch them. You can believe colorization will stop if the companies doing it start losing money. But if people decide they like such movies, who is to tell them that they don't have a right to see them?

What is ominous is the ease with which some people go from saying that they don't like something to saying that the government should forbid it. When you go down that road, don't expect freedom to survive very long.

The current crusade against men's clubs is another example of the idea that the anointed should decide whether something is good or bad, and then have the government impose their decision on others. If this destroys the right to get together with anybody you want to hang out with, the anointed don't care. When they are on a crusade, other people's rights don't matter.

The theory is that men's clubs provide opportunities to advance your career and promote your business, so it is unfair to keep women out. Now, if we are going to destroy someone's freedom every time someone else comes up with a theory, we may as well tear up the Constitution and forget it.

The kind of men's clubs the radical feminists are all worked up about think nothing of charging ten grand as an initiation fee. By the time you can pay that kind of money, your career is already pretty advanced. This is not how you get your first job out of college.

Shocking as it may seem in these enlightened times, men and women are different. The atmosphere and antics of all-male gatherings are different from mixed gatherings or all-female gatherings.

As a guest at one well-known men's club, I was struck by how much the evening's talks and skits by the members allowed some middle-aged men with heavy responsibilities to relax by acting like teen-age boys. It was hard to imagine a middle-aged woman enjoying it.

One radical feminist lawyer has even sued a women's health club for not admitting men. Why is it so important to stamp out every speck of difference?

Part of the reason is that all "movements" need a steady stream of grievances and victories. It doesn't matter whether the issue is large or small, real or phoney. At least it doesn't matter to them.

◆

THROWING MONEY—
AND INTERCEPTING IT

ONE OF THE REASONS why throwing money at social problems doesn't work is because someone is always there to intercept it.

Both in Milwaukee and in New York, for example, more than $6000 per child is spent on education annually. In both cities, less than half of that money ever reaches the school and less than a third is spent on classroom instruction.

That is one reason why pouring billions of dollars of the taxpayers' money down a bottomless pit has resulted only in American schools turning out some of the most expensive incompetents in the world.

Barely more than half the people employed by the New York City Board of Education are teachers. There are armies of bureaucrats, bureaucrats' assistants, and bureaucrats' cronies, on the payroll. Moreover, one third of the money that trickles down to the school goes for psychologists and counselors alone.

One of the great untold stories of our time is how psychologists have suckered so many people into thinking that shrinks are the cure for everything from losing the Super Bowl to coping with the "stress" of winning a lottery. But let's look at the bottom line: What has gotten better in American schools after we flooded them with psychologists, counselors, "facilitators" and the like?

Academic performance has certainly not improved. We have yet to see test scores as high as they were 30 years ago. It has been estimated that the average student's vocabulary today has less than half as many words as in 1945.

Maybe the students are happier, healthier, or something. But statistics on cheating, theft, vandalism, violent crime, venereal disease and teenage suicide all say no. At our leading colleges and universities, there is more racial strife than there was 20 years ago.

Educators are uncomfortable even discussing actual results. They are at their best talking a good game, full of lofty buzzwords and puffed-up jargon. As long as we keep buying it, they'll keep selling it.

Education is not the only area where throwing money at social problems results in very few completed passes. The federal government has been fighting a "war on poverty" ever since the days of Lyndon Johnson—and poverty is winning. It has been estimated that less than one-fourth of all the money spent on programs supposedly for the poor actually reaches any poor people.

Part of the money gets intercepted by bureaucrats, consultants, social workers, academic researchers and others who gather around these programs like flies around honey. More important, many programs are sold to the public as being for the poor, while the benefits spread to many middle class people, in order to build up an influential constituency to keep the programs going.

The assumption that spending more of the taxpayers' money will make things better has survived all kinds of evidence that it has made things worse. The black family—which survived slavery, discrimination, poverty, wars, and depressions—began to come apart as the federal government moved in with its well-financed programs to "help."

It's not a racial thing. In Sweden, where welfare state benefits have been far more widely available, for a much longer period of time, families are coming apart more so than in the United States. More than half the children born in Sweden are the result of unwed pregnancies.

You can destroy families in any group with welfare. In the United States, the destruction has been focussed on the poorer groups because the welfare has been focussed on the poor.

Today, we hear all sorts of people talking about how much money the government should spend to "solve" the homeless "problem." Ask yourself this question: How much gasoline must be sprayed on a fire to put it out?

Obviously, the gasoline is far more likely to make the fire larger. But the very possibility that we are feeding a fire, rather than extinguishing it, never seems to occur to those for whom the taxpayers' money is the magic answer to all problems.

You cannot subsidize irresponsibility and expect people to become more responsible. Many of those who say otherwise, who are urging us to throw more money at social problems, are among the organized hustlers out there to intercept it if we do.

◆

SPOILED BRAT POLITICS

A WOMAN AND HER SMALL SON were out walking, when they encountered a man who had some oranges. The man offered one of the oranges to the little boy, who snatched it and said nothing.

The embarrassed mother said: "Johnny, what do you say to the nice man?"

Johnny held the orange out and said: "Peel it!"

Many political movements today are very much like that little boy. It is the age of spoiled-brat politics. People who have contributed nothing to this society feel entitled to whatever is given to them—and demand more.

One of the social-activist ministers in San Francisco announced that his church would no longer accept donations of second-hand clothing for the indigent and the homeless. He insisted that they be given brand new clothing.

All over the country, various college student activists are demanding that their colleges hire more minority and female professors. Where these professors are to come from is not their problem. A recently published directory of black economists lists fewer than 500 people. That's less than one for every six colleges.

For mathematicians, engineers, and physicists, the picture is even more bleak—not just for blacks but for women, Hispanics, and American Indians, as well. The people just aren't there—not in the numbers required for group "representation." Even the spoiled brat who demanded that the man "peel it!" was asking for something that was possible. Academic spoiled brats don't even care if it's possible.

Those who are constantly demanding "safety" may sound more reasonable, but often what they are asking for cannot be delivered either. Some things can be made safer at a reasonable cost but others cannot. And some things cannot be made safer at any cost, because greater safety in one way creates more dangers in other ways.

This very paper you are looking at is not safe. Leave it in the wrong place and it can catch fire, starting a blaze that burns your house down—with you in it. Leave it in a crib and a little baby can try to eat it and choke himself. There are also perfectly wholesome and nutritious foods to which some people have a fatal allergy.

A mania for safety does not make the world safer. It just creates new and different dangers, often worse than the old. There are vaccines which save millions of lives but also infect a handful of susceptible people with a fatal dose of the disease.

Ban the vaccine because it isn't "safe" and there will be far more deaths. That has already happened with pesticides. The banning of DDT in a small Third World country like Sri Lanka almost immediately led to a quarter of a million new cases of malaria.

The biggest spoiled brats of all are the so-called "environmentalists," more accurately called the Green Bigots. Like all bigots, they think that what they want is all that matters, and what other people want doesn't count. If they have to jeopardize the livelihoods of a whole community, in order to save some reptile that most people have never seen, they will do it without hesitation.

Species have come and gone for millions of years, but now the Green Bigots want to bring this evolutionary process to a halt. Thank heaven there was no Sierra Club when the dinosaurs were around, or there wouldn't be any human beings today.

The hysteria of the moment among Green Bigots is "global warming." Just a dozen or so years ago, the hysteria was that we were heading for a new ice age. No doubt there will be yet another environmental political crusade a decade from now.

Crying "wolf" is a great way to get federal dollars for research, so it's not surprising that many scientists cried wolf. In addition, statistical fluctuations can be read different ways by honest scientists. But those scientists who didn't buy "global warming" were drowned out by the ruckus and only recently have the media finally begun letting them have their say.

What a number of scientists are saying is that a "global warming" disaster is baloney.

The Green Bigots have now shifted their tactics. They can't continue to pretend that "everybody knows" the Earth is warming disastrously. The new party line is that we dare not wait till we have solid evidence, because then it will be "too late."

Unfortunately, the very same argument could be used by those who claimed that we were heading for a new ice age. If we launch all sorts of multi-billion dollar programs and clamp down all kinds of government controls that wreck the economy—all in order to reduce the Earth's temperature—we could end up freezing even sooner.

There will always be spoiled brats as long as we cater to them. The time is long overdue for us to stop caving in to every group of self-righteous noisemakers.

◆

DANGEROUS GOVERNMENT

SOMEONE ONCE POINTED OUT THAT, while kittens may be cute, if they were 40 times larger, they would be some of the most dangerous things around. The federal government has never really been cute, but when it was a lot smaller, politicians and judges were not nearly as dangerous.

If there were stupid decisions, they were usually stupid decisions about things that didn't really matter very much to very many people. If there was corruption, then each taxpayer might lose a few cents or—at most—a couple of dollars.

But now we have such things as the savings and loan bailout, which can end up costing thousands of dollars for every man, woman, and child in America. For some families, that can be the difference between having breathing room and struggling to make ends meet. Government has reached a size where it is dangerous.

Down-sizing the government is not something that is going to happen overnight, if it happens at all. There is going to be a real struggle, just to keep it from growing bigger—and even that struggle is likely to be lost if we continue to have career politicians in Washington.

Someone has claimed that limiting politicians' terms in office would mean that we would lose the advantages of experience in public office. But what does political "experience" consist of, other than experience in creating illusions and deceptions? Congress has plenty of experience in preparing a federal budget every year, but they can't even get it completed on time—much less balanced.

There are literally thousands—if not millions—of people in this country who could get a federal budget completed on time, balanced, and with far less waste of the taxpayers' money. So could the people in Congress today, except that they are so preoccupied with being in Congress tomorrow that they are patsies for special interests.

The special interests are not going to go away. But you can pull their teeth by making their campaign contributions meaningless. That means not allowing politicians to be re-elected. One of the further benefits of that is that people in public office would no longer be career politicians but citizens taking time out from their regular careers to serve the country.

You could get a lot of genuine experience and expertise that way. With a few career scientists in Congress, it would be harder for organized hysteria to scare billions of dollars of the taxpayers' money out of the government to meet bogeyman dangers. With a few professional economists in Congress, it would be a lot harder to promote hysteria over the trade deficit, or "debtor nation" rhetoric, or Japan-bashing.

Can you see Congressman Richard Gephardt trying to snow Milton Friedman?

There are enormous numbers of public-spirited people who already donate their time to community organizations, who allow their homes to be used as polling places on election days, and who volunteer their services during times of natural disasters and other emergencies. There are plenty of people who would be willing to serve in Congress for a few years, without becoming a permanent ruling class who think of the people outside the Washington beltway as their subjects, or as guinea pigs for social experiments.

It is penny-wise and pound-foolish to limit the available supply of expertise and genuine experience from the real world by paying Congressmen salaries far below what first-rate professionals earn in law, medicine, engineering, or business, for example. If members of Congress were paid a million dollars a year each, that would add up to less than one-tenth of 1 percent of the federal budget—and less than $5 a year per taxpayer.

If you can get an honest Congress for the price of a six-pack, that's a bargain.

Even this small cost would be saved many times over by having a Congress no longer beholden to special interests who drain the federal treasury of billions each year. A hefty Congressional income and no re-election campaigns to finance would mean an end to a key source of corruption. Under these conditions it would make sense to have new laws forbidding anyone in Congress from taking any money from anybody else, under any conditions.

Would this kind of political reform be difficult? Of course. So have all previous changes been difficult. Impossible? Only if you think so and do nothing.

♦

AIDS TESTING

PEOPLE ARE ROUTINELY TESTED for a variety of diseases before getting life insurance, marriage licenses, or admissions as immigrants to the United States or other countries. Yet there is a shrill political outcry against adding AIDS to the list of dangerous diseases people are tested for.

Even when a blood sample has already been taken for other purposes, often you dare not test it for AIDS, under current laws and policies. This situation would be laughable, if it were not so utterly tragic.

AIDS has been made a unique exception to all the rules concerning fatal dangers to the public. Usually the over-riding principle is to err on the side of caution: "Better safe than sorry." But not with AIDS. From the time this disease was first discovered, the whole emphasis has been on protecting the AIDS-carrier from the public—not protecting the public from the AIDS-carrier.

The constant stream of sweeping reassurances about the ways you cannot get AIDS is part of this pattern. And when new ways of catching AIDS are discovered, the first order of business is to down-play the news, to prevent "hysteria."

Just a few short years ago, these confident experts who are continually reassuring us did not know that you could catch AIDS from blood transfusions. Within the past year, cases have surfaced where AIDS was transmitted by skin grafts. When a dentist and some health workers recently caught AIDS from their patients, this was once again down-played, on grounds that they had "breaks in the skin," through which the virus entered.

"Breaks in the skin" are not rare and exotic things. People scrape, nick, and cut themselves in innumerable ways, at home or at work. It is also easy to create a "break in the skin" by biting someone, as one child with AIDS has already done in school, and as a homosexual being arrested has already done to a policeman.

No other group of people afflicted with a deadly contagious disease are so politically organized. This is because homosexuals had their own "gay rights" organizations, law firms specializing in "gay" causes, and political action committees to put the pressure on politicians—all before AIDS was discovered. Homosexuals are also well-represented among intellectuals, entertainers, and others in a position to shape opinion.

Anyone who goes against the prevailing policies and dogmas on AIDS will be depicted in the media as a yahoo or a fascist—if such views are not suppressed altogether. However, two scientists with years of experience in AIDS research publicly opposed letting children with AIDS attend public school in New York. They of course got much less media attention than those who were saying what the media wanted to hear.

In this atmosphere, the authorities have only grudgingly backed into the most elementary steps to protect the public from AIDS-carriers. Even after it became known that AIDS could be transmitted by blood transfusions, there was hesitation and resistance to testing the blood in blood banks for AIDS. No one objected to this blood's being tested for hepatitis, but people with hepatitis are not organized. Testing for AIDS was politically controversial because gay activists tried to twist it into a "civil rights" issue.

The gay rights activists lost on that issue, but they have won on most others. More important, their perspective dominates the whole mindset with which this disease has been approached.

With other dangerous and contagious diseases, all sorts of efforts have been made to identify those carrying the disease, sometimes quarantining them, or otherwise trying to minimize their contacts with the general public. With AIDS, the approach has been diametrically the opposite. Every effort is made to conceal the identity of those who have AIDS, so that others cannot keep away from them.

The sacred buzzword is "confidentiality." The argument is that you don't want to drive AIDS patients "underground." But AIDS patients are already underground, as far as the public is concerned. Those who talk this way are doing their damndest to make sure we don't find out who the AIDS-carriers are in our midst.

Even when you somehow learn that someone has AIDS, newly passed "anti-discrimination" laws and policies make it harder for you to put distance between the AIDS-carrier and yourself or your children. In New York, for example, when a child with AIDS is admitted to a public school, not only is the child's identity kept secret, so is the identity of the school, to prevent parents from pulling their children out.

Again and again, the over-riding concern is to protect the AIDS-carrier socially from the public, not to protect the public medically from the AIDS-carrier.

In San Francisco, nurses were fired for wearing gloves or masks when treating AIDS patients. Washington policemen have been publicly denounced and ridiculed for wearing gloves when arresting homosexual rioters (known as "demonstrators" in the media). Yet when a dentist recently caught AIDS from his patient because he was not wearing gloves, no one reconsidered their condescending criticisms of nurses and policemen.

———————————————— ♦ ————————————————

DRUG ADDICTS AND
BUSYBODY ADDICTS

CRUSADERS LIKE TO TALK ABOUT "SOLUTIONS" but life is actually one trade-off after another. The only real question is: What are you prepared to give up in order to get what you want?

What would you be prepared to give up to get this:

1. An end to drug-related murders of policemen and of innocent by-standers in neighborhoods where drug wars take place.

2. A substantial reduction of the nation's prison population, relieving over-crowding and providing space to hold violent criminals.

3. An end to drug-financed corruption of law enforcement officials, including judges, and of politicians here and in foreign countries.

What would you have to give up to get all this? You would have to give up the attempt to run other people's lives, which is what our present drug laws are.

The morally anointed, whether liberals or conservatives, will never give up their attempts to tell other people what to do—and to get the government to impose their beliefs on others. But the rest of us ought to start thinking about the ever-growing cost of our futile drug laws and how the whole society seems to be unravelling as a result.

Bad as drugs are—and many of them are deadly—it is not the drugs themselves but the *illegality* of drugs that is corrupting individuals and whole communities. It is Prohibition writ large.

Just as Prohibition made illegal whiskey very profitable to organized crime, so prohibition against drugs is worth billions of dollars to criminals large and small, all across the United States.

What do people get out of using drugs? I don't know. I haven't even tried marijuana. But there is all the difference in the world between deciding that you don't want to do something and trying to force other people to live your way.

In an age where all sorts of busybodies want to "make a difference," we have to start counting the cost—in lives as well as in money.

When Prohibition was repealed, the two-bit criminals and big-time gangsters who were illegally manufacturing and smuggling whiskey went out of business. They couldn't compete with professional manufacturers.

Today's street criminals who make or sell drugs cannot compete with big pharmaceutical manufacturers, in price, purity, or safety. Neither can big-time drug smugglers pay off everybody between here and Colombia or Panama and still make a profit in competition with legal drug companies who don't have all those expenses.

Nothing will put organized crime out of the drug business faster than ending the illegality of drugs.

No one should kid himself that laws against drugs are stopping drug usage. Neither do spectacular drug busts, which do nothing but provide publicity for politicians and funerals for law enforcement officers. The amount of cocaine seized by federal agencies alone was 17 times higher last year than in 1981—and yet the amount that got through anyway was so great that the price has fallen.

This charade is not worth the money, the lives, or the corruption. What do we lose by getting rid of these laws that are a mockery anyway?

The worse case scenario is that some more people may take drugs. But the people who stay away from drugs today usually do so out of concern for their health, their safety, their self-respect, their family, and their future. Those are still big reasons to avoid the stuff, whether drugs are legal or illegal, whether the laws are enforced effectively or in the present atmosphere of sound and fury, signifying nothing.

What are the gains from repealing the drug laws, as we finally repealed Prohibition? By cutting the costs of drugs, we cut the incentives to commit the tremendous amount of crime currently necessary to support an expensive drug habit. In some cities, much of the robbery, burglary, mugging, and other crime is committed to get drug money. By trying to stop people from destroying their own lives with drugs, we are only creating incentives for them to destroy other people's lives to get the big money needed.

Some people are as addicted to being busybodies as others are addicted to drugs. We need to focus our attention on the rest of the population—the innocent victims of both—and repeal drug laws that produce bigger disasters than the ones they are trying to prevent.

◆

WHAT IS "CONSERVATISM"?

IF THERE IS ONE WORD I would like to see disappear from the English language, that word is "conservative." It doesn't really mean anything. Those Communists in the Soviet Union who believe in running the economy the old-fashioned Stalinist way are called "conservatives." Those Americans who believe in the opposite, free-market economy are also called "conservatives," though they have nothing in common with the Stalinists.

For years, Milton Friedman tried to use the term "liberal," in its original sense of a believer in individual liberty, as a label for his philosophy. For his trouble, he is now considered the world's foremost "conservative" thinker. Australia's Liberal Party still uses the word "liberal" in its original sense but they understand the need to translate for visiting Americans: "We would be considered conservative in the United States," they say.

One of the few people who continues to insist that he is a liberal in its original and true sense is Nobel Laureate Friedrich Hayek. In many circles, he is labelled an "ultraconservative."

"Conservative" is a strange word to use to describe people who want to make large and fundamental changes in the way the whole economy and society function. No President since Franklin D. Roosevelt has made more changes than Ronald Reagan. Some call it the Reagan Revolution. At the same time, he is considered the leading "conservative" political figure of this era.

Anybody who wants to continue moving in the same leftward direction we have been going for at least half a century is considered "liberal" or "radical," depending on how fast he wants to go. But anyone who wants to head off in a new and different direction is called "conservative"—even if what he advocates is something that has never existed before.

Milton Friedman, for example, has advocated vouchers instead of public schools, a negative-income tax to transfer cash directly to the poor instead of having bureaucracies hand out goodies, and a monetary system based on strict rules instead of the judgements of the Federal Reserve System. None of these things has ever existed in the United States. Yet Friedman is considered a "conservative," and is spoken of as if he is trying to go back to some earlier time.

Dividing people politically into "left" and "right," instead of liberal and conservative, doesn't really help clear up the confusion. Only the political left is really defined, even approximately. Everybody who opposes the left agenda is lumped together as "the right." Monarchists and democrats, libertarians and fascists, are all called "the right," even when they have nothing in common.

This view of politics is like the Ptolemaic view of the universe, with the earth in the center and everything else revolving around it. Today's political vision has the left in the center and everyone else defined by how they relate to the left. As one who thinks that most of what the left says and does is nonsense, I find myself labeled "conservative"—even though the only time I want to turn back the clock is when we go off daylight saving time in the fall.

Among the radical changes I would like to see are a Constitutional amendment that forbids anyone with income or wealth above the national average from receiving any government transfer payments. This one provision might be enough to balance the budget, by eliminating many billions of dollars of subsidies to non-needy people who just happen to be in certain industries, agriculture, or older age brackets.

I have nothing against "the elderly," especially as I am now becoming one of them. But we don't owe anybody anything just for living past a certain birthday. If people have run into some big trouble beyond their control, it's the decent and humane thing to do to try to help them, regardless of what their last birthday was. But pouring billions of tax dollars down a bottomless pit, just because people happen to fall into one social category or another is something else.

Other radical changes I would like to see include abolishing the office of Vice President, appointing federal judges for a fixed term instead of for life, and a line item veto for the President. It would also be good to elect Senators at large so that we would have the national interest represented in Congress, instead of just a lot of local interests.

None of these things has ever existed in the United States. But because they are not part of the left-wing agenda, they would be sure to be regarded as "conservative."

Oliver Wendell Holmes said that we should think about things, instead of about words. The time is long overdue to start thinking about specific policies, instead of about labels and rhetoric.

♦

"AHA!" STATISTICS

A STATISTICS TEACHER used to play a little game with his class. He would give them some simple experiments to do while he was out of the room. They were supposed to write down the numbers that came out of these experiments. They were also told to write down another set of numbers, made up out of their heads.

When the instructor returned to the classroom, he was supposed to guess which set of numbers was real and which set was phoney. Although the students tried their best to fool the teacher, he would usually just glance at the two sets of numbers and immediately tell them which set was real.

The students were baffled as to how he could tell. After a while, he finally let them in on the secret: The numbers they made up were too even, too orderly, too stable. Real statistics from the real world are seldom like that.

Real statistics are not even or orderly. They are irregular. They jump around or are lopsided.

It is a shame that this statistician didn't teach this lesson to the deep thinkers and the morally anointed in the media, in academia, in Congress, and in the courts. Whenever they see statistics that are uneven, or don't match their expectations, they conclude immediately that there is something wrong with the world—and they are off on another crusade.

Whenever people have a strong suspicion that something is so, any uneven numbers that are consistent with that belief are likely to be seized on and treated as heavy evidence. This is the "Aha!" school of statistics.

Back in the early days of World War II, for example, someone discovered that Japanese Americans were living concentrated near all sorts of military installations, railroads, power stations and other strategically important installations vulnerable to sabotage. Aha!

It was true—and you could not attribute this residential pattern to random chance. The conclusion was that Japanese Americans were positioning themselves to sabotage the American war effort against Japan. This belief played a role in the decision to round up Japanese Americans and ship them off to prison camps.

Only much later did cooler heads prevail and the facts come out. Japanese Americans, mostly farmers then, were living where they were *before* the strategic installations were built in these rural areas. Cheap land attracted these installations, as it had attracted the Japanese American farmers.

It wasn't random chance but it wasn't a plot either. Many things in this world are neither plots nor random chance—but they generate uneven statistics.

For decades, American anti-trust laws have been attacking "monopoly" on the basis of statistics. Whenever different human beings do the same thing, some do it better than others and lopsided statistics result. But a company that ends up with a conspicuously large share of the business in its industry or locality can find itself in a courtroom, being attacked by government lawyers and being heavily fined by a federal judge.

The real farce in many anti-trust cases is that the "monopolist" may be struggling to fight off his competition by the time the case is finally settled, after years of trials and appeals. The A&P grocery chain was once a repeated target of federal antitrust prosecutions, based largely on statistics about what "share of the market" it "controlled." All the while, competition from Safeway and other grocery chains took away the market share that A&P supposedly "controlled."

Today, newspaper "monopoly" is one of the trendy hysterias, based on statistics showing that many towns and cities have only one newspaper published locally. Aha!

In reality, you can find more newspapers than ever before, in even the dinkiest little town out in the boondocks. Half a dozen newspapers from major cities are sold in Oakdale, California (population 10,000) and even in Yosemite Valley. The Wall Street Journal has a printing plant in Palo Alto, a couple of blocks from the Stanford campus and 3,000 miles from Wall Street.

Technological advances in communications and transportation make it economically feasible to sell far more newspapers in a given community than those produced locally. It is not necessary to read a Palo Alto–based newspaper, even to find out what movies are playing in Palo Alto. The San Francisco Examiner publishes that information.

Yet all it takes to maintain the hysteria are anti-trust zealots with statistics and judges who either share the same vision or are gullible enough to be bamboozled by numbers. The same formula works in many employment discrimination cases, where you can't find a single woman or minority member who has personally been discriminated against by the particular employer—but where the statistics don't please the judge.

In recent years, courts have started backing away from heavy reliance on statistics by themselves as showing employment discrimination. This has set off hysteria in Congress, leading to a bill sponsored by Senator Ted Kennedy and Congressman Gus Hawkins, which will make "Aha!" statistics the law of the land.

◆

"AHA!" STATISTICS (No. 2)

ALMOST ANY STATISTICS you can think of will fluctuate over time—from batting averages in baseball to the Dow-Jones average in the stock market. The prices of strawberries, gasoline, pocket calculators and cameras all fluctuate over time, as will attendance at movies, rainfall in California, and volcanic eruptions.

At any given time, statistics also tend to be uneven. Minnesota supplies more than its share of hockey players, just as California supplies more than its share of baseball players, and Pennsylvania and West Virginia more than their share of miners. Phoenix gets about twice as much sunshine as Seattle and Babe Ruth used to hit more home runs in some seasons than some whole teams that he played against.

Despite all this, some of the great hysteria and wild political crusades of our time have grown out of the simple fact that numbers fluctuate or are lopsided.

When the average temperature in the world goes up or down a few degrees for a few years, the hysteria and the hype begin in the media. Back in the 1970's "a new ice age" was predicted. In the 1980's just the opposite was predicted. "The greenhouse effect" became the new buzzword. It is supposed to produce "a global warming trend" that threatens all sorts of disasters.

Any scientist who wants to add his voice to the hysteria will be featured on television and quoted in *Time* magazine, which is leading the environmentalist stampede on this issue. Any scientist who says it is baloney will be ignored, like someone who is trying to spoil a party. A number of scientists, both in the United States and in other countries, have said that it is baloney but neither the media nor the politicians want to hear that.

What they want to hear are things that make for excitement, crusades, and a chance to be the side of the angels. They want statistics or anything else that blames our whole way of life for creating catastrophic dangers that only the wise and noble few can save us from.

Whether it is "the greenhouse effect," chemical residues from pesticides, the dangers of nuclear radiation, or a thousand other things, the bottom line is the same: The morally anointed are to stand on Olympus and order the rest of us around—for our own good.

Statistics that ruin this scenario are seldom mentioned. For example, all the carbon monoxide put into the atmosphere by the entire human race has been estimated as less than one-fifth of what is put into the atmosphere by volcanoes alone. Natural pesticides produced by plants put many times more cancer-causing chemicals into our bodies than all the man-made pesticide residues in the world. Nuclear radiation from nature likewise overwhelms the tiny amount of radiation created by man.

Once we realize that human actions are only a small part of a much bigger global picture, we can begin to understand the fraudulence of the propaganda by the anointed who are just itching to run our lives for us. It is not just the so-called "environmentalists"—or "green bigots," as they are more accurately described. All sorts of social statistics are manipulated for the same purpose of gaining more power to boss people around.

A common ploy with social statistics is to extrapolate from some trend to show what disaster it will lead to. Decades ago, fancy mathematical models were used to show how economic growth would grind to a halt by the 1980's. In reality, the 1980's turned out to have one of the strongest sustained periods of economic prosperity in history.

Clever statistical extrapolations don't mean anything unless you understand the reality that generated the numbers. No doubt the temperature has risen since dawn today. And if we were to extrapolate this rise we would project temperatures that would burn us all to a crisp before the end of the month. It is only when we realize that the rising temperature was caused by the earth's spinning us into the sunlight that we realize how the same spinning will take us out of the sunlight again and cause temperatures to drop.

Unfortunately, the growth of statistics, the development of theories, and the availability of computers to play games with it all has led too many people to regard these mathematical manipulations as a substitute for knowing what they are talking about. Even more unfortunately, this has also provided yet another way for political crusaders to push their hidden agendas under the guise of "science."

◆

"AHA!" STATISTICS (No. 3)

IN AN ELECTION YEAR, especially, we can expect to hear a lot of reckless rhetoric. A lot of reckless numbers will also be thrown around. Unfortunately, neither the public nor the media has developed as much skepticism towards numbers as toward words.

Perhaps the most damaging use of numbers is to "prove" discrimination against women, minorities, or other groups through statistical disparities. This assumes that there is something unusual about statistical disparities, or that they can be explained only by discrimination. In reality, great statistical disparities are common in virtually everything that people do, even in situations where discrimination is out of the question.

Over the past several years, six times as many men as women have been struck by lightning in the United States. In the Soviet Union, the consumption of cognac was 8 times as high per capita in the Baltic as in Soviet Georgia.

There are countries where a racial or ethnic minority has earned several times as many college degrees as the majority, even though the minority has no control over the university or the government. This was true of the Chinese in Malaysia for the entire decade of the 1960s. It was also true of the southern Nigerians at about the same time, even though the majority of the population of Nigeria lived in the north.

In Fiji, where the number of descendants of immigrants from India has been roughly equal to the number of indigenous Fijians, the Indians received several times as many degrees at the university as the Fijians, who have been dominant in the government.

Here we are talking about several times as many degrees in absolute numbers.

Countries where racial or ethnic minority degree-recipients have been "over-represented" by several times, relative to their percentage of the population, are too numerous to mention. They include Asians in the United States, Tamils in Sri Lanka, Japanese in Brazil, and Jews in numerous European countries.

It has likewise been common in countries around the world for racial or ethnic minorities to own the overwhelming majority of firms in whole industries. Again, there isn't space enough to list them all, but they have included Greeks in the Ottoman Empire, Italians in Argentina, the Lebanese in Sierra

Leone, the Chinese in Indonesia, and the Germans in France, Brazil, and Russia.

In India, two groups of the same race, religion, and language performed so differently, whether in farming the same land or in taking the same civil service tests, that the Andhras repeatedly surpassed the Telanganans by embarrassingly large margins. Eventually the Telanganans resorted to riot, arson, and looting, and a constitutional crisis was provoked before the political situation could be stabilized.

A mere listing of the times and places where particular minorities have dominated particular occupations—including highly paid occupations—would literally fill volumes. Even minorities known to have been discriminated against have dominated various well-paid occupations. One need only turn on a television set and watch basketball games to see that that is true in the United States today.

The reasons behind all these huge statistical disparities are as wide-ranging as the disparities themselves. Sometimes these reasons can be traced back through history, but for other disparities, there is scarcely a clue.

Despite voluminous evidence to the contrary, politicians and even judges solemnly discuss statistical disparities as equivalent to "inequities" and "discrimination."

There is no doubt that discrimination is among the many reasons for statistical disparities. The fatal fallacy is in reasoning backwards from numbers to guilt. It makes lawsuits easier, but is that the purpose of law?

The tragedy of so-called "affirmative action" is that it cannot even be discussed rationally. Neither logic nor evidence escapes being brushed aside impatiently. There are grown men and women who seriously believe that bad motives are the only possible reason why anyone could disagree with them on this issue.

It is considered morally repugnant—"divisive" is the bogeyman word in politics and the media—to discuss publicly this public policy that is building up enormous resentments across the country. If respectable people refuse to talk about it, that only adds to the credibility of people like David Duke who break the silence and get a monopoly on the issue to exploit politically.

The deep and needless tragedy in all this is that the surface appearances of affirmative action are radically different from the underlying reality.

"Quotas" are a focal point of the discussions on both sides, when quotas are not even half the story. The huge legal liabilities created by policies that make statistical "under-representation" equivalent to discrimination create incentives for employers to protect themselves by putting distance between their companies and those communities from which they can expect large numbers of minority applicants.

Minorities may lose far more jobs from the location choices of employers than they will ever gain from quotas, and yet the quotas will still generate great bitterness among others. Even whites who would never have been hired, if the business had been located somewhere else, will resent the fact that their friends or relatives didn't get hired because of quotas.

The era of affirmative action has not seen any speeding up of the progress of blacks. On the contrary, this has been precisely the era when the historic economic advancement of working-class blacks has begun to fizzle out, and when an underclass seems to have become an enduring part of inner-city life.

Affirmative action has been a great boon to minority elites in the United States, as it has been a boon to elites in other countries around the world. As long as the elites define the issues, affirmative action will be like an operation that is considered a success, even as the patient is dying.

◆

"AHA!" STATISTICS (No. 4)

"WHERE YOU FROM, STRANGER?" they used to ask in the old Westerns.

It is a question we ought to ask today about many of the statistics that are thrown around to convince us that there is some "crisis"—and to stampede us toward somebody's pet "solution." Many of these statistics are from organizations that stand to get more money and power, and a bigger empire, if they can get the public alarmed.

The first thing to remember about most statistics about national issues is that they seldom come from actually counting individual people. Usually, they come from taking a sample and then making projections based on various assumptions and definitions. What those assumptions and definitions are make all the difference in the world.

If it is the Census Bureau estimating the population or the Gallup Poll testing political sentiment, the estimates are probably based on reasonable assumptions and definitions. But when the agency or organization making the estimates has a vested interest in getting the public alarmed, the assumptions and definitions are likely to reflect that fact. The resulting statistics are often gullibly accepted by the public and the media alike, even when these numbers are as phoney as a three-dollar bill.

Currently, two of the biggest areas of statistical hype are hunger and illiteracy. One widely-cited study of hunger defined "hungry" people as those who are eligible for food stamps but don't get them. This definition produced millions of "hungry" people. It also produced the "hungriest" county in the United States—a farming and ranching area with low money income but only two people receiving food stamps. It didn't matter if people in this county were eating their own home-grown food, or even chowing down on steaks. Statistically, they were "hungry."

The mere fact that people are lining up for free food is "proof" enough to some that there is widespread hunger. If the government or private agencies started handing out free shoes, people would undoubtedly start lining up for them. But that does not prove that vast numbers of Americans are barefoot.

As long as you are willing to give handouts to people on the streets, there will be people on the streets to take handouts, whether in money or in kind. Even the lowest unemployment rates in more than a dozen years will not get people off the streets, if they are getting money for being on the streets.

Real hunger is a real problem. I have had some personal experience with being hungry, and do not recommend it to anyone. But the statistics that are being thrown around to stampede the public and the politicians have little relationship to hunger. Television can always dig up a hungry person to put on the screen and tell a sad story. But hand-picked examples don't legitimize phoney statistics—or shouldn't.

The same game is played with "illiteracy" statistics. The percentage of Americans who are illiterate ranges from less than one percent to more than 30 percent, depending on whose statistics you choose to believe. The media choose to believe far bigger statistics, which arouse more alarm and therefore create bigger TV ratings.

Some of the big "illiteracy" numbers come from presenting people with something written in bureaucratic gobbledygook. When they can't make heads or tails of what it means, they are declared "illiterate" for purposes of the statistical study—and for political purposes. The media often fall in line with this, by presenting someone who is genuinely illiterate, and treating his situation as if it is typical.

The next time you see some alarming statistics, ask as they did in the old Westerns: "Where you from, stranger?"

◆

"IMPOSSIBLE"
POLITICAL REFORMS

POLITICS IS CALLED "THE ART OF THE POSSIBLE." But the political eras and
the political leaders that are remembered introduced changes that would
have been impossible before.

The Reagan revolution of the 1980s would have been impossible 20 years
earlier. Franklin D. Roosevelt's New Deal innovations of the 1930s would
have been considered madness a decade earlier. Just 5 years ago, anyone
who predicted all the changes set in motion by Mikhail Gorbachev would
have been urged to seek psychiatric help.

Most professional politicians are preoccupied with what is politically
feasible right now. Even the great innovators usually take ideas that have
been around for a while and have gradually gotten enough acceptance to be
worth a try. Without the ideas of Milton Friedman and others in the 1960s,
Ronald Reagan could not have moved this country—and the world—in the
direction of a free market in the 1980s.

What are some of the political ideas we should be thinking about today,
in hopes that they will become possible in the 21st century?

The Achilles heel of democratic societies has been their short-sighted-
ness. Stupid and even dangerous policies have been promoted by leaders
who knew better, but who were responding to fashionable political moods or
to the pressures of the moment. Contrary to appearances, there are some
very intelligent people in Washington. The country doesn't get the benefit
of their intelligence because they are worried about being re-elected.

Some people think "an informed public" is the answer. It would help.
But there is no way that anyone can be really informed about all the incredible
range of things the federal government is doing—not as long as we have 24-
hour days and people have to work to make a living.

What we need in government are men and women who can use their
talents to make better decisions for the country, rather than to get themselves
re-elected. That is, we need to replace career politicians with people from
all sorts of other walks of life, people who will serve in government for a few
years to give the country the benefit of their experience and wisdom, gained
in the real world beyond the Washington beltway.

There are a few such people in government right now. But the problem is that they are under the control of career politicians. The supply of conscientious and knowledgeable people is large enough to replace the political hacks in government. There are innumerable people who donate their time to serve on all sorts of community organizations and on national organizations such as the Red Cross or the American Cancer Society. The question is: How can we get such people to replace career politicians in Congress and elsewhere?

As long as re-election is the guiding star of government decisions, there will continue to be short-sighted, parochial, stupid and dangerous decisions. As long as campaign contributions are essential to raise the millions of dollars required to be re-elected, special interests will continue to contribute millions to Congressmen—and to get back billions of dollars of the taxpayers' money in return, courtesy of Congressmen who vote all sorts of subsidies and boondoggles.

How can this vicious cycle be broken? One way to make the career politician impossible is to ban re-election. Congress has already limited the President of the United States to two terms. Logically, it is a short step from there to limiting Congressmen to one term in office.

Politically, of course, it is a very long step to start recycling Congressmen back to the real world when they want to remain big pooh-bahs in Washington. But few important policy reforms were feasible when they first began to be discussed.

If we want an entirely different kind of person in political life, we are going to have to make it possible for people who have succeeded in the real world to put aside lucrative careers without sacrificing the education of their children or the well-being of their families. Nothing is more penny-wise and pound-foolish than the present practice of skimping on the pay of people who control enormous sums of federal money.

Washingtonians speak blithely of spending "billions" on this or that program, or of a total federal budget exceeding a trillion dollars. Does anyone have any idea how vast those sums are? A billion seconds is more than 30 years. A trillion seconds ago, no human being on this planet could read or write.

If we paid every Congressman a million dollars a year, it would amount to less than one percent of the federal budget. That could be more than made up the first year by dropping federal subsidies to special interests, to whom Congress would no longer be beholden.

PART V
THE EDUCATION SCENE

EXCUSE TIME

"THE WORST CONTINUED TO WORSEN," John Kenneth Galbraith said, in his entertaining account of the stock market crash of 1929. Unfortunately, that also applies to American education today.

Recently released statistics show that American high school students have now reached an all-time low in their verbal scores on the Scholastic Aptitude Test, taken by more than a million young people preparing to go on to college. Looking back over the past 30 years, the highest S.A.T. scores were reached in 1963, the entire decade of the 1970s saw declines every year, and the minor improvements of the 1980s never reached the levels achieved 20 years earlier. Now the 1990s have begun with a new decline. The worst continues to worsen.

With years of experience in dealing with bad results, the educational establishment has become expert at explaining them away. The first line of defense is that the results don't mean anything. A favorite variation is that American colleges are now providing "access" to so many "disadvantaged" students that of course the average scores of those applying to college are a little lower.

Unfortunately for this argument, test scores have been declining *at the top*. Twenty years ago, more than 116,000 students scored above 600 (out of a possible 800) on the S.A.T. Today, with slightly more students taking the test, fewer than 75,000 score that high. In math, about the same proportion score above 600 as in 1971. However, we must remember that 1971 was not a golden age. The decline was already under way for several years by then.

When declining results on a wide variety of tests cannot be talked away, educators then argue that this shows a need for more money to be spent on the public schools. Thus the tables are turned and "society" is put on the moral defensive for having "neglected" the education of the next generation by not "investing" enough in their education, condemning them to "overcrowded classrooms" and the like.

In reality, the United States spends more money per pupil than most other nations, including nations whose youngsters consistently outperform ours on international tests. We spend more money than Japan, for example, whether measured in real per pupil expenditures or as a percentage of our Gross National Product. We have fewer pupils per class than Japan, and in mathematics our classes are less than half the size of Japanese math classes. The only thing we don't have are results. American students have come in last in international math tests.

"Society" has not failed its children. The public schools have failed. That is what all the clever evasions and distractions seek to conceal.

There is really nothing very mysterious about why our public schools are failures. When you select the poorest quality college students to be public school teachers, give them iron-clad tenure, a captive audience, and pay them according to seniority rather than performance, why should the results be surprising?

Money is not the problem here, either. Better-qualified people become private school teachers at lower salaries. The crucial problem is with the filter through which the overwhelming majority of teachers pass—education courses. Mediocrity and incompetence pass readily through such filters, but education courses repel more able and intelligent college students. Paying higher salaries to the kind of people who emerge from this process only makes mediocrity and incompetence more expensive.

It is not simply the dullness or the shallowness of education courses that is crucial, nor is it simply the academic deficiencies of the people who choose to take these courses. Rather, it is the fatal attraction of *non-academic* projects to people for whom academics have never been a source of achievement or pride. Throughout this century, there has been an on-going struggle between laymen trying to focus the public schools on teaching academic subjects, while the educators have increasingly gone off into the wild blue yonder of endless non-academic fads.

While students in Japan are studying math, science and a foreign language, American students are sitting around in circles unburdening their psyches (and family secrets) in a wide range of psycho-babble courses called "affective education." What with "nuclear education," multiculturalism, environmentalism and a thousand other world-saving crusades, our students are learning to "express themselves" on all sorts of issues for which neither they nor their teachers have even the rudiments of competence.

It is going to be difficult to get teachers who are even academically oriented, much less academically able, as long as education courses are the legally mandated filter through which the vast majority of teachers pass. Such courses are legal prerequisites solely because of the political muscle of the education establishment, whose top priority is preserving the jobs of its own. Forty million American school children are thus sacrificed to preserve the jobs of fewer than 40,000 professors of education. That's more than a thousand youngsters sacrificed for every education professor.

◆

MINORITY
COLLEGE STUDENTS

MANY YEARS AGO, when I was teaching at Howard University, a black institution in Washington, D.C., a very dispirited young man came to my office
after he had received a "D" on an examination in my economics class.

"I don't know how I could have done so badly, Mr. Sowell," he said, with
a sincerely puzzled look on his face. "I studied so hard before the exam. Do
you know, I studied for TWO HOURS for that exam!"

I didn't know whether to laugh or cry.

The student looked even more puzzled when I told him that two hours
was just a warm-up period to begin some serious studying. His eyes widened
when I said that I spent more than two hours preparing a one-hour lecture
on a subject I had taught before—and had studied for ten years before that.

Later, this incident made me think back to my own student days, when
I was a freshman at Howard. I always thought of myself as a hard-working
student and so did others around me. But, after I transferred to Harvard at
the beginning of my sophomore year, my room-mate there said to me one
day:

"When are you going to stop goofing off, Tom, and get some work done?"

I was stung by the accusation. Goofing off! What was he talking about?

When my first mid-term grades arrived, they were half D's and half F's.
What would have been good work, by the standards I was used to, was
considered goofing off at Harvard. A faculty adviser called me to his office
and told me, in effect, that I would have to shape up or ship out.

I began to pay attention to how my room-mate worked. Nort was a math
major and it was not unusual for him to start struggling with his math
assignment in the mornings, right after returning from class. I could hear
him muttering and cursing under his breath as he worked over the problems.

At noon, we often had lunch with our third room-mate, Ralph, a physics
major with an almost straight-A average. They would sometimes talk about
various mathematics principles that might give a clue as to how to attack
some tough problem.

In the afternoon, the assault on the math problems continued. A whole
page of calculations might be crumpled up in anger and thrown into the

waste basket, after it became clear that that particular approach led into a blind alley. Somewhere around mid-afternoon, Nort would cry out:

"WAIT A MINUTE! I've got it!"

That usually meant that he had finally penetrated to what the real problem was, and now it was just a matter of turning out a few equations that led to the answer. He too was an almost straight-A student and today is chairman of the math department at a prestigious eastern college.

Between my grades and my room-mates, I realized that my work habits had to change. Studying now meant burning the midnight oil until I mastered my assignment. If it took until 2 or 3 A.M., then that was what it took.

Today, when a master of ceremonies introduces me as someone who graduated with honors from Harvard, I think back to those days and the introduction seems a little misleading. It is true that I graduated with honors—but only after a lot of dust had settled.

There is nothing surprising about the fact that many students who come from schools with lower standards, or from families where no one has ever gone to college, do not really understand what is required for first-rate work at a first-rate institution. In an earlier era, it was understood that they would simply have to shape up or ship out. Most of them shaped up.

Today, on too many campuses, there are too many people offering too many excuses and too many cop-outs for minority students. Their academic problems are blamed on "cultural bias" in the courses, "the white power structure," or a lack of "role models." Nobody has the guts to tell them to shape up or ship out. The net result is that more of them end up shipping out.

◆

BRAINWASHING IN SCHOOL

SOME PEOPLE MAY HAVE BEEN SHOCKED when they saw a recent report on "death education" on the television program "20/20." Among other things, the program showed high school students being taken to morgues to touch dead bodies.

Was this just some kooky teacher's idea? Not at all. This is part of a whole nationwide movement. Your local high school may have it—even if the parents don't know about it.

In fact, this is just one of many emotional manipulations of children that go on in public schools across the country—behind the backs of parents.

One mother who visited a classroom in a little town in Colorado found the students seated in a circle (very common in these fad programs) and one little girl crying. It was a discussion group and the question of the day was: "Who died last in your family?"

The little girl's grandfather had died.

"Death education" starts early in some schools. In one Florida county, first-graders were given an assignment to make their own coffins out of shoe boxes. In a Massachusetts school, eighth-graders had an assignment to write a suicide note.

A very common practice is to assign students to make choices as who is to die in a situation where everyone cannot be saved—in an overloaded lifeboat, for example. Some schools require students to decide which member of their own family must die, when the whole family cannot be saved.

Some children have emotional reactions to school programs that constantly harp on death. Some cry in class, some have trouble getting to sleep at night, or have bad dreams. Others have committed suicide—and though their parents have blamed "death education" programs, there is no way to prove it in court.

"Death education" is only the tip of the iceberg. There is a whole spectrum of courses and programs designed to brainwash children into rejecting the values, beliefs, and ways of life taught them by the parents—and to accept the latest fad thinking on subjects ranging from death to sex to social philosophies in general.

Whatever the particular subject matter, these programs follow standard brainwashing techniques of putting the victims under emotional stress, breaking down their inhibitions, and destroying their links to others on the outside.

With school children, the link that must be loosened or broken is the child's link to his or her parents. In innumerable ways, some very subtle, these programs undermine, ridicule, or otherwise sidetrack parents as irrelevant. Sometimes children are explicitly told not to tell anyone—including their parents—what is said in the "magic circle," as these classroom brainwashing sessions are often called.

When the subject is sex rather than death, the underlying technique is the same. Breaking down inhibitions is the first order of business. For example, a parent who visited a fifth grade class in Oregon reported:

"I was present when a plastic model of female genitalia with a tampon insert was passed around to the boys so they might understand how tampons fit."

How important was such information to eleven-year-old boys? Not very. But the real question is: How important is it to brain-washers to break down inhibitions? It is crucial.

That is why so-called "sex education" courses go on for years in some schools. It doesn't take that long to convey the facts of life. But it does take that long to relentlessly undermine what the children have been taught at home.

Breaking down inhibitions takes many forms. Movies showing close-ups of childbirth have been shown in elementary school (even though one child fainted in a North Carolina classroom). Movies showing sex—all kinds of sex—have been shown in high schools. Questionnaires about the students' own sex lives have been passed out in high school.

One girl, who was reluctant to use the word "penis," was forced to say it loudly—10 times—in class.

Then there are the "peace studies" or "nuclear education" programs where the horrors of war are presented so graphically and so relentlessly that many children are reduced to tears. One teacher told her seventh-grade students that "no one in this class will be alive in the year 2000."

What all these programs have in common is that zealots are out to promote their own fads or causes to a captive audience of vulnerable children. The emotional well-being of these children is not their problem.

How do they get away with it? Deception is crucial. These programs are called by such nice-sounding names as "health education," "values clarification," "drug prevention," "decision-making," or even "gifted and talented" programs.

What parents would refuse permission for their children to get the benefits of things with such nice names as these?

Back in 1984, the U.S. Department of Education held hearings in various parts of the country on such brainwashing practices. Although the government never published these hearings, Phyllis Schlafly collected much of the testimony in a book called *Child Abuse in the Classroom.*

It should be required reading for every parent.

——————————————————— ♦ ———————————————————

THE ECONOMICS OF ACADEME

ACADEMIA IS BIG BUSINESS—or at least big money. More than 20 universities receive over $100 million each annually from the federal government alone. Johns Hopkins receives more than half a billion. In addition, 10 institutions have their own endowments in excess of a billion dollars. Harvard has over $4 billion.

Then there are alumni contributions which add up to about $5 billion for private institutions and about $2.5 billion for public colleges and universities. Finally, there is tuition, rising faster than the rate of inflation for the 8th consecutive year.

Tuition in five figures used to make us gasp but Bennington College now charges more than 15 grand a year and it barely manages to retain the "honor" of being the most expensive college in the country. Add room and board, books and transportation, and you will be lucky if it comes to less than $20,000 a year at many colleges and universities.

What is the country getting for all this money?

One thing the country clearly does *not* get is gratitude, or even loyalty. Harvard takes 123 million federal dollars a year but refuses to allow a Reserve Officers Training Corps on its campus. There are Harvard students who want to be in R.O.T.C. but they have to go to M.I.T. for it. This contempt for the military that makes their survival and freedom possible is not limited to Harvard.

What of the education that the colleges and universities are providing, with the help of billions of federal dollars and billions in private donations?

One of the signs of our times was a certain momentary shock, a couple of years ago, when a newspaper story said that Brooke Shields graduated from Princeton without taking a single course in mathematics, history, chemistry, economics, physics, or biology. This was not special treatment for Brooke Shields. Nor was Princeton unique in allowing students to graduate without some of the basic understanding that marks an educated person.

There are colleges from coast to coast where anyone can get a degree without bothering to get an education. Superb educations may be available at some of these institutions—but you don't have to get one if you don't feel like it. Just pay the tuition, put in your four years, and walk out with an embossed piece of paper to prove that you were there.

That is not the worst of it. An increasing number of professors, courses, and whole programs are devoted to propaganda for particular ideologies, rather than being devoted to the intellectual development of students. At one time, the proud motto was: "We're here to teach you how to think, not what to think." More and more courses today are there to teach you what to think. And, if you don't know how to think, so much the better.

Those students who want to think for themselves, to question or even challenge the professor's conclusions, are likely to get put down or marked down in many propaganda courses. This is especially likely in the "studies"— women's, ethnic, peace, or environmental. But ideological intolerance is not uncommon, even in traditional subjects. A student in an English course at the University of Michigan had her grade reduced for writing "Congressman," instead of the professor's ideological preference, "Congressperson."

Professors who are true believers do not hesitate to publicly embarrass any student who does not follow the party line. This kind of thing has been tolerated so long and so widely that some profs openly state that their courses exist to promote a particular ideology, even though they collect a paycheck for teaching.

A history professor at the University of Massachusetts declared: "I am biased. I'm not going to give you both sides of every question." His course, he promised, "will be consistently anti-American."

Despicable as this may be, it is at least candid. But even candor is lacking in the many attempts by Stanford University to deny that its surrendering its Western Civilization course to the demands of anti-Western ideologues was a political capitulation rather than an educational decision. It was not even a controversial judgment as to whether particular books by particular non-Western writers were better than Plato or Shakespeare.

Neither the books nor the professors to teach the new course had been selected when Stanford caved in to demands based on the race and sex of the new and still unknown authors. Not since Hitler talked about "German mathematics" and "German physics" have the social origins of authors taken such precedence.

No. Americans are not getting their money's worth from their colleges and universities. And writing more blank checks will not help.

◆

QUOTAS AGAINST ASIANS

A PROFESSOR OF ENGLISH at one of the better eastern colleges was appalled at the low quality of the essays her students turned in. In order to get them to understand what an essay should be like, she xeroxed one of the few good ones and gave a copy to each student.

It was an essay written by a Vietnamese student who learned to speak English only 5 years ago.

Asian students have had so many remarkable academic success stories that we are no longer surprised. What should be surprising—in fact appalling—is that some people seem to think they are *too* successful. Evidence is growing of quotas being used to limit the number of Asians admitted to some top colleges and universities.

Congressman Dana Rohrbacher of California has been trying to dig out the facts about quotas being used to limit the number of Asian American students admitted to colleges and universities. He has also been trying to light a fire under the Office of Civil Rights at the U.S. Department of Education, to get them to take legal action against such discriminatory practices.

In keeping with its general policy of not rocking the boat in academia, the Department of Education is proceeding with all deliberate slowness.

According to the Department of Education itself, the Law School at Berkeley maintained racially separate waiting lists of applicants throughout most of the 1980s. In 1989, after Congressman Rohrbacher and others made a public issue of quotas against Asians at Berkeley, the Berkeley Law School discontinued racially separate waiting lists. According to the Department of Education, there is now "a unitary waiting list"—even though this "unitary" waiting list shows "the race or ethnicity of students who were to receive special consideration."

What a revolutionary change!

You know and I know that if any such practices had been used to keep out women or a number of other minorities, other than Asians, all hell would have broken loose. Instead, the Department of Education says it will "conduct a compliance review" and that this review "will be scheduled as soon as possible." They don't say it will *begin* as soon as possible. But they will pencil it in on the schedule.

None of this necessarily indicates an animosity toward Asians, either at Berkeley or at the Department of Education. The animosity is much broader than that, and extends far beyond college campuses. The hostility is against rewarding outstanding performance and productivity.

Wherever the criterion is performance rather than body count, Asian Americans are usually "over-represented." That means you cannot have the statistical representation of all groups in proportion to their percentage of the population if you use performance as a criterion. Any high-performance group upsets the plans of those who think it is their prerogative to mix and match different groups to present a pretty public relations picture.

In an earlier era, the problem was how to keep out Jews—another high-performance group that upset the preconceived notions. Today, that problem has disappeared because Jews are just lumped in as part of "whites." Asians have, in effect, inherited the anti-Semitic quotas of the past.

This whole issue is broader and deeper than anti-Asian quotas. It is part of a fundamental conflict between those who believe in rewarding productivity and those who believe in handing out rewards as "entitlements" just for being around. By and large, believers in entitlements have been winning that conflict—especially in academia. Individuals, groups, or nations whose performances have earned high rewards are treated as if they were guilty of something.

Many people are poor because they were not born into circumstances that encouraged them to develop productive skills or attitudes. Whether this was due to family history or group history, such children have a bleak future, unless they can be encouraged or required to develop basic skills as they grow up. Instead, they are often told bogeyman stories about how their problems are all due to being "exploited" or "excluded" by their more fortunate contemporaries. These bogeyman stories are often the work of intellectuals as well as politicians.

When high-performance Asian Americans show up, they ruin this whole political morality play. Asians have experienced a history of discrimination but their high performance today shows that that is not the only factor that counts. Their history threatens the whole ideological house of cards, on which many people's federal grants, careers, and egos are based.

No wonder that quotas against Asians arouse so little concern. But we should all be concerned, not only about Asian Americans, but about what happens to performance in a country that downgrades performance.

‹◆›

"SEX EDUCATION" FRAUD

THERE WAS A RECENT FLAP in New York City over first-grade textbooks about "daddy's room mate" and a girl who "has two mommies." Both books were designed to accustom first-graders to the idea of homosexual parents.

The flap was over one school district that objected, not all the other districts that quietly accepted this re-making of social values as a role for the public schools. Even in the one unwilling school district, some objected only that the first grade was too early for this kind of thing.

Much of this missed the point. What are American public schools doing getting into such things in the first place? Do they have time and energy to dissipate in ideological crusades to re-shape the values of other people's children, when educators are failing miserably to convey the academic skills they are being paid to teach?

No small part of the reason why American school children fall so far behind their contemporaries in other countries in international comparisons of educational achievement is that Japanese and other youngsters are studying math, science, and other solid subjects while our children are being brainwashed with the latest ideological fashions—whether about homosexuality, environmentalism, multiculturalism, or a thousand other non-academic distractions.

Too many critics have allowed themselves to be drawn off on a tangent to discuss the merits or demerits of these particular ideologies. The more fundamental objection to teaching this stuff is that we are not sending our children to school to have their values and psyches re-molded to suit ideological zealots on world-saving crusades. It is cheap, cowardly, and dishonest to target children—and especially to do so behind the backs of their parents.

Let these crusaders pick on somebody their own size, instead of taking advantage of children who were entrusted to their care for entirely different purposes.

Few parents or citizens realize the pervasiveness of classroom brainwashing, or the utter dishonesty with which it is smuggled into the schools under misleading labels.

Does anyone ask himself why it should take years and years to teach school children so-called "sex-education"? Obviously it does not. What takes years and years is to wear down the values they were taught at home and lead them toward wholly different attitudes and wholly different conceptions of the world.

Brainwashing takes time—and it takes this time away from academic subjects.

First-grade textbooks promoting homosexual lifestyles are only the opening salvo in year after year of assaulting children's values. The issue is not homosexuality or the relative merits of traditional versus avant-garde beliefs. The issue is: *Whose children are these?*

By what right do other people usurp the responsibilities of parents and use the schools to carry on guerilla warfare against the values that parents have taught their children?

Sex education is just the tip of the iceberg. There is, for example, also "death education," which often includes excursions to morgues, funeral homes, and graveyards—as well as classroom exercises in which children are asked who should live and who should die (including members of their own families) when a lifeboat is too overcrowded to hold everyone.

What is the purpose of all this? Whether the subject is sex education, death education, environmentalism, nuclear power, or innumerable other ideological issues, the purpose is to impose the attitudes, values, and world outlook of the anointed on other people's children.

The zealots know what they are doing, and are well aware of its illegitimacy. One teacher's manual for a widely-used program includes instructions on how to evade parent's complaints and how to deal with students who don't go along.

A mother who complains individually is almost certain to be told that she is the only one who has ever objected. There may be controversies raging from coast to coast, and even lawsuits filed over the program, but you will still be told that you are the only one who has complained.

Complain in a group and the cry will be "censorship." The education establishment knows how to play the game of heads-I-win- and-tails-you-lose.

To the media, each program is an "innovation" to be judged in isolation—and usually not very critically. They do not understand that each program, which may seem only questionable in isolation, is part of a much larger brainwashing effort—and it is that distortion of the whole purpose of American education which is truly outrageous.

Clausewitz said that war was the continuation of politics by other means. Too many people in the education establishment, at all levels, treat education as the continuation of ideological crusades by other means.

The glib gurus who set the trends are at war with all the fundamental values of this country and this civilization. You would have to know these people, or read their writings, or see their "art," to understand the venom in their hatred. To such people, our children's education is a small sacrifice on the altar to their vision.

---- ◆ ----

THE FUTURE OF ACADEME

"THIS IS S. O. TERRICK, science reporter for your eyewitness news team. I am reporting from the Packet Inn, located out on Moot Point, overlooking Dyer Straits. We are here covering the celebration of a momentous event. Here with me to explain is Professor Murky of Ivy University."

"Thank you. We are all here to celebrate a scientific breakthrough by one of our physicists at Ivy University. I am spokesperson for the inter-disciplinary team that will be studying its applications."

"Just what is the breakthrough, professor?"

"We now have a time machine that can retrieve objects from the past or the future."

"A time machine! You mean I could go back and interview Julius Caesar or —————."

"No, no. It hasn't yet reached the point where it is safe for human beings to go through the stress of time travel."

"Oh. So you couldn't send Miss Manners into the twenty-first century to see what customs will be like then?"

"No. Such a trip would be especially stressful for her, since she is living in the eighteenth century as it is."

"Well, what sort of objects can you bring back to the present with this time machine?"

"I thought we should try to get an idea of the most advanced thinking of the future by bringing back a catalogue of Ivy University a hundred years from now."

"Sorta get an idea where current academic trends are leading. Right, professor?"

"Exactly. Now here's the college catalogue of the future, fresh out of the time machine."

"Wow! What's it say?"

"Well, for example, here's a philosophy course of the twenty first century.

The catalogue says, 'PHILOSOPHY 106: Non-Judgemental Thinking. This course explores the scientific incorrectness and social inappropriateness of words like right and wrong. Historical figures like Attila the Hun, Ivan the Terrible and Adolf Hitler are re-examined in the light of this philosophy.'"

"I see. What else is in store for the future?"

"Well, some of the courses are still pretty conventional. For example, here's HISTORY 215: American Foreign Policy. Covers the period from President Theodore Roosevelt's philosophy ("speak softly and carry a big stick") to the period of Secretary of State George Shultz's philosophy (speak loudly and carry a little stick). The course will compare how these two approaches worked out differently in Panama."

"Yes, that is pretty conventional. Do they have other courses that show newer trends in thinking, professor?"

"Oh yes, many. For example, here is POLITICAL SCIENCE 300: Change by Disruption."

"What's that all about?"

"The catalogue description says: 'A study of how old-fashioned methods of policy through elected representatives has been superseded by disruption as a means of fostering social change. The class project this semester will be to set fire to a government building and dynamite the headquarters of a multinational corporation.'"

"That's really getting down to the nitty-gritty, Professor Murky."

"Yes. It shows the depth of their commitment to progress."

"Professor, we have time to discuss just one more course before we return to the studio. Do you have another good one for us, to show how the thinking of the next century will be so much more advanced than our traditional ideas today?"

"Oh, yes. Here's one in my own field—SOCIOLOGY 101: Hit Persons."

"Hit persons?"

"It's obviously what we today call 'hit men.' But the more advanced language of the future will avoid sexist labels."

"Hit men? You mean hired killers?"

"That's a pejorative term that will not be used in the more progressive society of the future. The course description in the catalogue says: 'A non-judgemental study of hit persons—the stresses of the occupation, the dangers, the difficulties of selecting the appropriate ammunition, the stigma attached to the occupation by society, and how this stigma victimizes hit persons.'"

"That's really breath-taking. Wait a minute, professor. What's that piece of paper that fell out of the catalogue?"

"It's some kind of official announcement. Let me see. It says that all classes have been cancelled for the rest of the academic year."

"Why?"

"Some students have set fire to the classrooms, dynamited the administration building and shot half the professors."

"That's too bad."

"The announcement says that when these students are caught, we must
remember to be non-judgemental and to offer them counseling."

◆

UNSUNG HEROES

THOSE WHO THINK THAT THIS is an era without heroes may not be looking
in the right places.

Certainly there are few heroes to be found along the banks of the Poto-
mac, and many ivy-covered campuses are scenes of some of the most abject
cowardice to be found anywhere, as college administrators have turned
surrender to strident demands into a fine art.

Ironically, however, some of the most heartening signs of courage are
also to be found on many college campuses. Students who publish unofficial
college newspapers, challenging the imposed ideological conformity known
as "diversity," do so at risk to their social acceptance, their academic standing,
and even their physical safety. These unsung heroes are a major source of
information about the internal corruption of American higher education.

Occasionally, the national media get a glimpse of the ideological intolerance on campus when some well-known public figure is prevented from
speaking by the storm trooper tactics of a cadre of student activists—who are
seldom either resisted or punished by the college administration. But, in
many other instances, where neither the occasion nor the speaker is such as
to attract reporters, similar or worse things may happen without anyone off
campus realizing what is happening.

When a black student at Vassar College unleashed a torrent of anti-
Semitic abuse at a campus gathering there a few years ago, the school's
administration was far more interested in hushing up the incident than in
punishing the student. Only the courage of the students who published *The
Vassar Spectator* brought this disgrace to public attention, despite pressure
from the college administration to squelch the story.

The whole apparatus of campus thought control known as "political correctness" was first exposed by unofficial college newspapers, sometimes known as "conservative" newspapers (with varying degrees of accuracy). Only after their many horror stories began to be picked up by journalists in the mass media did this become a public issue.

As an industry whose image is its bread and butter, because of its heavy dependence on outside sources of money, academia maintains a tight control on what information will be allowed to reach the public, and with what "spin" put on it. Such public relations products as alumni magazines or college press releases will never betray any secrets that would jeopardize private donations or government grants.

It took federal investigations to ferret out Stanford's widespread misuse of government grants for campus perks.

The official college newspapers are unlikely to expose ideological double standards and campus thought-police at work, simply because the students who work on such papers are almost invariably of the dominant ideology themselves. That is why it was necessary to establish unofficial student newspapers in the first place.

College administrators are masters of public relations, whatever their deficiencies as educators, and they have understood from the outset the danger that unofficial student newspapers represent—and have repeatedly tried to suppress, impede, or intimidate them. On some campuses, only the issuance of court orders has stopped administrators from interfering with the distribution of these unofficial student newspapers. At the University of California at Davis, the conservative paper can only be distributed at a remote location, well removed from where the officially approved papers are made available.

Increasingly stringent speech codes at colleges across the country make normal journalistic criticisms hazardous to students who write for unofficial campus newspapers. Objections to double standards for minorities, women, or homosexuals are often equated with "racism, sexism, and homophobia"— charges which can bring on a variety of punishments, including suspensions and expulsions.

Being a student-journalist on a conservative campus newspaper has other hazards as well.

Some professors have not hesitated to denounce these students in the classroom—sometimes with obscenities—for what they have written in their newspapers. Cries of "fascist" as they walk across campus, anonymous death threats, and an occasional rock or bottle thrown through a window—these are all part of the experience of students writing for conservative campus papers.

Another common experience is being depicted as rich, white male racists—even when these newspapers have been run by women editors, by black editors, or by Asian editors, each of whom has been in charge of *The Dartmouth Review* at one time or other. The publisher of *The Princeton Tory* described herself as the first member of her family to go to college and the editorial staff of *The Vassar Spectator* has been characterized as mostly first- and second-generation Americans.

Desperate efforts to destroy or discredit unofficial or conservative campus newspapers are a testimonial to their crucial importance in letting the public know what college administrators don't want us to know.

◆

STUDENTS AS PAWNS

THE CALIFORNIA SUPREME COURT RULED last week that students in the University of California system cannot be forced to contribute money to political or ideological organizations.

If you think that this is an issue that should never have come up in the first place, then you may not know that student fees are still being used to contribute to ideological crusades on campuses all across the country.

In the majority opinion written by Justice Edward Panelli, the California Supreme Court said, "Students are, in fact, forced to support causes they strongly oppose." For the state to force students to do that seems so obviously wrong that it seems incredible that it was done, or that there was any question that it should be stopped.

However, two of the Justices dissented from the majority and one wrote that such compulsory contributions were "germane to the university's educational mission" and even served "compelling national interests."

A student leader who wanted the involuntary "contributions" to continue said: "This would be a significant blow to students' ability to present opinions to the Legislature and the regents."

Obviously, there would have been no case in the first place if students all wanted to give money to subsidize political lobbying. Turning some students into "the" students is an old verbal game.

Unfortunately, this judicial ruling affects only state institutions in California. State colleges and universities in other states, and private institutions across the country, remain free to commandeer their students' money to be donated to whatever political or ideological causes are in vogue on campus.

A whole movement has been supported financially by money siphoned out of college students' pockets. These are called by the pious name of "Public Interest Research Groups" (P.I.R.G.s) and their ideology is essentially the ideology of Ralph Nader.

Whether students agree or disagree with that viewpoint, their student fees include money to be contributed to the cause. These P.I.R.G.s are scattered across the country, under the name CalPIRG in California, MassPIRG in Massachusetts, ConnPIRG in Connecticut, and so on.

At one time, CalPIRG collected more than $57,000 a year from student fees at U.C.L.A. and more than $124,000 a year from student fees at Berkeley. On the east coast, a local PIRG collected hundreds of thousands of dollars a year from the various campuses of Rutgers University. It speaks volumes about the mindset of those who run these and other institutions that they saw nothing wrong about using the students as pawns in this way.

Only when the regents finally cracked down did this particular practice stop in the University of California system. It took a lawsuit to put a stop to this rake-off at Rutgers. But the practice still flourishes elsewhere.

Unfortunately, this is only one of many ways in which students are treated as pawns at all levels of the educational establishment, from the elementary schools to postgraduate institutions. Moreover, money is only one of the objectives.

Brainwashing is one of the major objectives in schools and colleges alike. Many critics have complained about the particular ideas that the students are being brainwashed with—whether on homosexuality, animal rights, or a thousand other trendy issues—but the more fundamental problem is brainwashing itself.

Even if all the notions that students are being brainwashed with were 100 percent true, memorizing other people's propaganda is not learning how to think for yourself.

Even if all the "politically correct" answers were the right answers, the questions themselves are sure to change with the passing years—and if you haven't learned to think for yourself, a collection of right answers to yesterday's questions is not going to help.

Even today, with American students trailing behind students in many other countries academically, how do our schools have the luxury of wasting their time on fashionable ideological crusades? Why are we teaching about homosexuality to children who can't even spell the word?

The answer is that the ideological fashions have so gripped so many "educators" that education itself is seen as a continuation of politics by other means. Students are perfect targets because they are vulnerable: They are young, they are inexperienced, and they are at the mercy of those who hand out the grades.

Zealots are seldom troubled by the fact that what they are doing is cowardly in picking on people whose minds are not yet developed enough to defend themselves. Nor are they ashamed of the dishonesty of doing such things behind the parents' backs and under misleading labels.

When "educators" do not hesitate to treat students as pawns, that is a reason why all the rest of us ought to be very concerned, very angry—and ready to fight to put a stop to it.

◆

STUDENT LOANS

THE FIRST LESSON OF ECONOMICS IS SCARCITY: There is never enough of anything to fully satisfy all those who want it.

The first lesson of politics is to disregard the first lesson of economics. When politicians discover some group that is being vocal about not having as much as they want, the "solution" is to give them more. Where do politicians get this "more"? They rob Peter to pay Paul.

After a while, of course, they discover that Peter doesn't have enough. Bursting with compassion, politicians rush to the rescue. Needless to say, they do not admit that robbing Peter to pay Paul was a dumb idea in the first place. On the contrary, they now rob Tom, Dick, and Harry to help Peter.

The latest chapter in this long-running saga is that politicians have now suddenly discovered that many college students graduate heavily in debt. To politicians it follows, as the night follows the day, that the government should come to their rescue with the taxpayers' money.

How big is this crushing burden of college students' debt that we hear so much about from politicians and media deep thinkers? For those students who graduate from public colleges owing money, the debt averages a little under $7,000. For those who graduate from private colleges owing money, the average debt is a little under $9,000.

Buying a very modestly priced automobile involves more debt than that. And a car loan has to be paid off faster than the ten years that college graduates get to repay their student loans. Moreover, you have to keep buying cars every several years, while one college education lasts a lifetime.

College graduates of course earn higher incomes than other people. Why, then, should we panic at the thought that they have to repay loans for the education which gave them their opportunities? Even graduates with relatively modest incomes pay less than 10 percent of their annual salary on the loan the first year—with declining percentages in future years, as their pay increases.

Political hysteria and media hype may focus on the low-income student with a huge debt. That is where you get your heart-rending stories—even if they are not at all typical. In reality, the soaring student loans of the past decade have resulted from allowing high-income people to borrow under government programs.

Before 1978, college loans were available through government programs only to students whose family income was below some cut-off level. That cut-off level was about double the national average income, but at least it kept out the Rockefellers and the Vanderbilts. But, in an era of "compassion," Congress took off even those limits.

That opened the floodgates. No matter how rich you were, it still paid to borrow money through the government at low interest rates. The money you had set aside for your children's education could be invested somewhere else, at higher interest rates. Then, when the student loan became due, parents could pay it off with the money they had set aside—pocketing the difference in interest rates.

To politicians and the media, however, the rapidly growing loans showed what a great "need" there was. The fact that many students welshed when time came to repay their loans showed how "crushing" their burden of debt must be. In reality, those who welsh typically have smaller loans, but have dropped out of college before finishing. People who are irresponsible in one way are often irresponsible in other ways.

No small amount of the deterioration of college standards has been due to the increasingly easy availability of college to people who are not very serious about getting an education. College is not a bad place to hang out for a few years, if you have nothing better to do, and if someone else is paying for it. Its costs are staggering, but the taxpayers carry much of that burden, not only for state unversities and city colleges, but also to an increasing extent even for "private" institutions.

Numerous government subsidies and loan programs make it possible for many people to use vast amounts of society's resources at low cost to themselves. Whether in money terms or in real terms, federal aid to higher education has increased several hundred percent since 1970. That has en-

abled colleges to raise their tuition by leaps and bounds and enabled professors to be paid more and more for doing less and less teaching.

Naturally all these beneficiaries are going to create hype and hysteria to
keep more of the taxpayers' money coming in. But we would be fools to keep
on writing blank checks for them.

When you weigh the cost of things, in economics that's called "trade-
offs." In politics, it's called "mean-spirited." Apparently, if we just took a
different attitude, scarcity would go away.

♦

MULTICULTURAL MADNESS

MOST OF THE ARGUMENTS for so-called "multicultural" education are so
flimsy, inconsistent, and downright silly that it is hard to imagine that they
would have been taken seriously if they were not backed up by shrill rhetoric,
character assassination, and the implied or open threat of organized disruption and violence on campus.

Let us examine the multiculturalists' questions, one by one:

Why do we study Western civilization, to the neglect of other civilizations?

Why is that question asked in English, rather than in some non-Western
language? Because English is what we speak. Why do we concern ourselves
with the Earth, which is an infinitesmal part of the known universe? Because
that is where we live. If we want to understand the cultural and institutional
world in which we carry on our daily lives, we need to understand the
underlying rationale and the historical evolution of the way of life we have
been born into.

None of this has anything to do with whether English is a better language
than some other languages. English is in fact more inconsistent and less
melodic than French, for example. But we speak English for the same
practical reasons that cause people in China to speak Chinese. Attempts to
turn this into an invidious comparisons issue miss the fundamental point that
(1) languages exist to serve practical purposes and (2) they serve those purposes better, the more people in the same society speak the same language.

Why don't we study other civilizations equally? The most obvious answer
is the 24-hour day and the limited number of days we spend in college. It is

stretching things very thin to try to cover Western civilization in two semesters. Throw in a couple of other civilizations and you are just kidding yourself that you are educating anybody, when all that you are really doing is teaching them to accept superficiality. Those whose real agenda is propaganda are of course untroubled by such considerations.

Any suggestion that any aspect of Western civilization has been admirable, or better in any way than the corresponding aspect of any other civilization, will of course be loudly denounced as showing bias instead of being "non-judgmental." However, the one thing that no civilization has ever been is non-judgmental. Much of the advancement of the human race has occurred because people made the judgment that some things were not simply different from others, but better. Often this judgment was followed by abandoning one cultural feature and using the other instead.

We use Arabic numerals today, instead of Roman numerals, even though our civilization derived from Rome, and the Arabs themselves got these numerals from India. Arabic numerals (or Indian numerals) have displaced other numbering systems around the world because they are better—not just different. Paper, printing, and books are today essential aspects of Western civilization, but all three came out of China—and they have displaced parchment, scrolls, and other forms of preserving writings all around the world. Books are not just different, they are better—not just in my opinion, or in the opinion of Western civilization, but in the practice of people around the world who have had an opportunity to make the comparison. Firearms have likewise displaced bows and arrows wherever the two have come into competition.

Many of those who talk "non-judgmental" rhetoric out of one side of their mouths are quick to condemn the evils of "our society" out of the other side. Worse, they condemn American society or Western civilization for sins that are the curse of the human race all across the planet. Indeed, they condemn the West for sins that are worse in many non-Western societies.

Perhaps the classic case is slavery. The widespread revulsion which this hideous institution inspires today was largely confined to Western civilization a century ago, and a century before that was largely confined to a portion of British society. No one seems interested in the epic story of how this curse that covered the globe and endured for thousands of years was finally gotten rid of. It was gotten rid of by the West—not only in Western societies but in other societies conquered, controlled, or pressured by the West.

The resistance put up by Africans, Asians, and Arabs was monumental in defense of slavery, and lasted for more than a century. Only the overwhelming military power of the West enabled it to prevail on this issue, and only the moral outrage of Western peoples kept their governments' feet to the fire politically to maintain the pressure against slavery around the world.

Of course, this is not the kind of story that appeals to the multiculturalists. If it had been the other way around—if Asian or African imperialists had stamped out slavery in Europe—it would still be celebrated, in story and song, on campuses across America.

Why are the traditional classics of Western civilization written by dead white males?

Take it a step at a time. They are written by dead people for two reasons: First, there are more dead people than living people. Second, a classic is not something that is hot at the moment but something that survives the test of time. There may be things written today that will survive to become classics, but we won't be here when that happens. The things we know are classics were almost by definition written by dead people.

Why were they white? Do we ask why the great classics of China were written by people who were Chinese? If we found that the great classics of China were written by Swedes, wouldn't we wonder what the hell was going on?

Should there be any mystery as to why they were written by males? Is anyone so utterly ignorant of history that they do not know that females had more than enough other work to keep them busy for most of the history of the human race? Maybe men should have shared some of that work. But history is what happened, not what we wish had happened. If most of the people who were educated were male—as they have been throughout history, and even today in some societies—then most of the people who leave the kind of written material left by educated people will be men. You don't get great mathematical discoveries from people who were never taught algebra.

Much the same reasoning applies to other groups considered to be (1) oppressed and (2) "under-represented" among those whose historic achievements and contributions are recognized. But how can a people's achievements be unaffected by their oppression? One of the many reasons to be against oppression is that it keeps people from achieving all that they could have achieved if they had been treated more decently. To proclaim oppression and stil expect to find the oppressed equally represented among those with historic achievements and contributions is almost a contradiction in terms.

The past is many things, but one thing it is, is irrevocable. A past to your liking is not an entitlement.

Don't we need multiculturalism to get people to understand each other and get along with each other?

Since this is an empirical question, you would expect people to seek an empirical answer, but most of those who talk this way seem content to treat the matter as axiomatic. But is there any evidence that colleges that have gone whole hog into multiculturalism have better relations among the various groups on campus? Or is it precisely on such campuses that separatism and hostility are worse than on campuses that have not gone in for the multicultural craze?

You want to see multiculturalism in action? Look at Yugoslavia, at Lebanon, at Sri Lanka, at Northern Ireland, at Azerbaijan, or wherever else group "identity" has been hyped. There is no point in the multiculturalists' saying that this is not what they have in mind. You might as well open the floodgates and then say that you don't mean for people to drown. Once you have opened the floodgates, you can't tell the water where to go.

How are we to be part of the global economy, or engage in all sorts of other international activities, without being multicultural?

Ask the Japanese. They are one of the most insular and self-complacent peoples on Earth today. Yet they dominate international markets, international finance, international scientific and technological advances, and send armies of tourists around the world. This is not a defense of insularity or of the Japanese. It is simply a plain statement of fact that contradicts one of the many lofty and arbitrary dogmas of multiculturalism.

PART VI
THE LEGAL SCENE

"VIEWS" VERSUS INTEGRITY

MANY YEARS AGO, a black professor—a militant on racial issues—was teaching a course in economics at a well-known university. Among his students were two white South Africans.

"Now, I hate those bastards," he told me. But it turned out that the South Africans were the two top students in his class, so he gave them an A and an A +. That is what integrity is all about.

Such integrity is the hallmark of professionalism, whether in a professor, a physician or a judge. That is what makes it so wrong-headed for members of the Senate Judiciary Committee to be grilling nominees for the Supreme Court about where they "stand" on "issues." Any Justice of the Supreme Court who decides cases on the basis of where he personally stands on issues lacks the integrity for the job.

Justice Oliver Wendell Holmes made no secret of the fact that he despised some of the people in whose favor he voted. One he accused of writing "a silly leaflet," based on a "creed of ignorance and immaturity." Holmes was quite clear about the role of a Supreme Court Justice. His job was "to see that the game is played according to the rules," he said, "whether I like them or not."

It has taken centuries of struggle by giants to establish the ideal of "a government of laws and not of men." Today, pygmies are trying to reduce it all to a question of a judge's "views" on some "issues," whether he will be a "champion" of this or that group, or of this or that cause.

To listen to the confirmation hearings on Judge Clarence Thomas, you would scarcely guess that Judge Thomas had written a number of decisions on the Circuit Court of Appeals, and had voted on more than a hundred other decisions there. Were those decisions good, bad, or indifferent? No one seemed to be nearly as interested in that as they were in what he said in a speech at some political gathering, years ago. These statements were supposed to provide clues to his "views."

In recent years, judicial confirmation hearings have become more and more like a Roman circus, complete with Christians being thrown to the lions. Whatever their ratings as political theater, such hearings are a serious and lasting disservice to the country.

Above all, they promote a dangerous misconception about the role of courts and the rule of law. Where a judge "stands" on "issues" is far less important than where he stands on judging.

If a nominee has already been a judge, then it is his record as a judge that should be scrutinized—not to see whether everyone agrees with his decisions, but to see whether those decisions reflect faithfulness to the written law, intelligence in applying the law, and the integrity to keep his own personal emotions out of it.

The dry application of legal rules may not be very exciting stuff, but it is crucial to the survival of freedom. In a free society, people know in advance what the rules are—and they know that they are not subject to arbitrary power, so long as they stay within those rules. You cannot have a framework of known rules if judges are free to engage in legal adventures, based on their own personal philosophy.

To ask judicial nominees where they "stand" on "issues" is to suggest that this should be the basis for their rulings. If it is, then there will be as many different versions of the law as there are judges—and freedom will become a memory.

Another dangerous long-run consequence of turning judicial confirmation hearings into political theater is that some of the finest legal minds in the country cannot be nominated to the Supreme Court. Their writings, instead of being evidences of the kind of intellect sorely needed, become a "paper trail" for committee staff aides to comb through to find a word here and a phrase there, as targets for political grandstanding by the Senators.

Under these conditions, the qualities needed to survive confirmation hearings are radically different from the qualities needed to become a first-rate Supreme Court Justice—and we cannot risk having second-rate Supreme Court Justices.

Finally, the badgering, the cheap shots, and the innuendoes that have become standard procedures in judicial confirmation hearings in recent years not only demean the individual nominee but undermine the dignity of the high office itself.

When a question has been asked once, and answered either satisfactorily or unsatisfactorily, nothing further is gained by asking it dozens of times more in different words. Some nominees have had their integrity questioned in Senators' opening statements, before saying a word. Senators have votes with which to express their opinions. They do not need to have insults as well.

Public respect for the courts and the law is one of those intangibles, without which all the tangibles are not going to work.

——————————————— ◆ ———————————————

THE ANTI-TRUST PICTURE

IF YOU MET ALEX KOZINSKI SOCIALLY, and tried to guess his occupation, probably the last thing you would think was that he was a judge. Witty and playful, Kozinski is also as sharp as a razor when it comes to cutting through nonsense.

Judge Kozinski was thus the perfect man to write the opinion when another ridiculous antitrust case came before the 9th U.S. Circuit Court of Appeals. It was the old story: Some businessman was successful enough to have an expanding share of the total sales in his market and the feds wanted him convicted of monopolization.

This particular businessman owned movie theatres in Las Vegas—and Judge Kozinski is a movie buff. The opinion he wrote for the Court of Appeals was full of phrases like "top gun," "little big man" and "against all odds." Someone counted over 200 movie titles used as phrases in Kozinski's decision!

The decision itself, however, was not only serious but profound. It showed a far deeper understanding of economics than many ponderous Supreme Court decisions that talked nonsense in pompous language. Judge Kozinski's clever presentation will make this decision a classic that will be read by many more people. It should be.

The Justice Department's Antitrust Division tried to use the statistical approach that has suckered other judges in the past. The local theatre owner had built so many theatres, and bought so many from his rivals, that he ended up showing 100 percent of all first-run movies in Las Vegas. Back in the olden days, that would have made a conviction for monopolization as automatic as a point after touchdown.

Kozinski blocked this kick, however. No statistic—not even 100 percent—means anything unless you understand the process from which it came and the reality that gives it meaning. Far from having a monopoly, the first-run theatre chain soon found that one of the second-run theatre chains in Las Vegas was now beginning to show first-run movies. In just three years, the former second-run chain was showing more first-run movies than the "monopolist" whom the Justice Department was prosecuting.

As Judge Kozinski noted, "market share at a particular time" is not the be-all and end-all. It can be a very misleading predictor of the future, if you take seriously the claim that a business "controls" the percentage of the market that it has for the moment. If a business cannot prevent rivals from coming into the market to compete, then it does not have any economically meaningful monopoly, no matter what the statistics say.

The Justice Department's lawyer spoke ominously of "the monopoly power" of the Las Vegas movie chain and went into the kind of bogeyman theories that have won antitrust cases in the past. But Judge Kozinski, "rejecting the government's argument," found "no indication that competition suffered in the Las Vegas movie market," where the defendants obviously "lacked the power to exclude competitors."

Judge Kozinski also put his finger on a broader problem in government policy—that agencies claiming to offer "solutions" must constantly find "problems," to justify their own existence, whether a problem really exists or not. Kozinski said: "It is a tribute to the state of competition in America that the Antitrust Division of the Justice Department has found no worthier target than this paper tiger on which to expend limited taxpayer resources."

Too many judges have let themselves be bamboozled by too many numbers—and not just in antitrust cases. Not understanding the complex processes from which these numbers were generated, judges have been patsies for bogeyman theories by clever lawyers. Often the judge's own vision of an evil society, needing the intervention of the anointed, has led to court decisions that made no sense and caused endless mischief.

By ridiculing the ridiculous, Judge Kozinski has fulfilled a very serious duty. Perhaps his decision will help bring us closer to the time when bogeyman theories will be gone with the wind.

◆

SUPREME SECOND-GUESSERS

MUCH OF WHAT SOPHISTICATES loftily refer to as the "complexity" of the real world is in fact the inconsistency in their own minds. Nowhere is this more true than in the U.S. Supreme Court.

In the recent case of *Hudson v. McMillian,* 7 Justices got themselves tangled up in self-imposed complications over the Eighth Amendment's ban on "cruel and unusual punishments." A handcuffed prison inmate had been beaten by prison guards. That was certainly cruel and we must hope that it was unusual. The real question is whether it was punishment.

When the Constitution was written, punishment referred to the sentences meted out in court—not the subsequent administration of prisons. For more than a century and a half, courts respected this clear meaning, which is to say, they respected the boundaries of their own power. Then, during the recent decades of judicial self-indulgence, all sorts of new meanings were read into the Constitution.

In 1976 the legal concept of "punishment" was extended beyond its historic meaning in the Eighth Amendment. The administration of prisons was now transformed into a constitutional issue.

No doubt many terrible things happen in prison—and always have. This is not one of those new, modern "complexities" which supposedly "force" the courts to adapt a "living Constitution" to our more advanced times. Those who wrote the Constitution simply had the good sense not to try to make it cover every sparrow's fall.

Every misdeed, outrage, or even atrocity is not unconstitutional. It is still not unconstitutional to murder the President of the United States, for example, and 30 years ago it was not even a violation of a federal statute. Yet, in recent decades, the dangerous idea seems to have gained acceptance that whatever shocks a Supreme Court Justice is unconstitutional.

Justice Sandra Day O'Connor, who delivered the Court's decision in *Hudson vs. McMillian* referred to "evolving standards of decency that mark the progress of a maturing society" to justify judges' rushing in where the Constitution gave them no authority to tread. She was quoting a 1981 decision—which is to say, she was following the logic of extensions of the Constitution breeding new extensions.

Worse, it breeds a pervasive uncertainty as to what laws in general mean. That is good news only to lawyers. Centuries of struggle, agony, and bloodshed have gone into promoting the ideal of "a government of laws and not of men." Now all of that has been blithely waved aside with lofty talk about "evolving standards"—which means that you cannot know what the law means until judges issue the latest bulletin from the "evolving standards" front.

Why did the Constitution establish other branches of government, if not to allow changing needs and standards to be reflected in changing laws and policies? Too often the "evolving standards" of the judges are simply the *zeitgeist* of the anointed imposed on an electorate which has rejected it.

You cannot have a law-abiding society unless people know—in advance—what the law means. Not only individuals but institutions cannot be decisive when "evolving standards" turn judges into roving second-guessers with power, rather than enforcers of known laws.

Schools are paralyzed in dealing with disruptions and violence that threaten the very purposes for which schools were established, because no one knows how some judge will apply "evolving standards" and let the school be sued by a hoodlum who was expelled. Businesses, foundations, and public agencies likewise live in the shadow of murky "evolving standards" of law, which ultimately mean that even the most clearly spelled out law or contract does not protect you from some judge's crotchets.

The so-called "litigious society" is not unrelated to the judicial blurring of legal lines. Judges have created many of the troubled waters in which lawyers fish. More important than the particular damage awards, or the legal blackmail that leads to out-of-court settlements, is the indecisiveness imposed on decision-makers in general.

Put differently, those who know—who are on the scene and have the experience, training, and expertise to realize what needs to be done—are constrained by the second-guessers with their "evolving standards." Those who know are being stifled by those who don't know.

What is at issue are not simply the particular facts of the particular prison episode on which the Supreme Court ruled in *Hudson v. McMillian*, but the legal principles they resorted to in resolving that case. It is not easy to remain faithful to the written Constitution and at the same time respect the legal precedents of an era when earlier judicial adventurers have gone off into the wild blue yonder.

That is not due to "complexity," however. It is due to the legal inconsistencies inherent in trying to make the Constitution an instrument of the *zeitgeist* instead of a framework for a government of laws and not of men.

--------------------------------- ◆ ---------------------------------

SUPREME CHUTZPAH

THE U.S. SUPREME COURT has once again come to the rescue of the wrongos. Now 5 Justices have suddenly discovered that the Constitution will not permit a murderer to be executed, because he was 15 years old when he committed the crime.

My copy of the Constitution doesn't say that. Nor has any previous Supreme Court discovered any such implication in nearly 200 years of analyzing the Constitution. But today Justice John Paul Stevens rushes in where Oliver Wendell Holmes feared to tread.

In contrast to the clear, concise, and penetrating opinions that were the hallmark of the great Justice Holmes, Justice Stevens' opinion for the Court is a rambling mishmash of pop psychology, fashionable social ideology, and political speculation. Someone who committed a premeditated and calculatedly sadistic murder escaped execution because of what Justice Stevens calls "the unambiguous conclusion that the imposition of the death penalty on a 15-year-old offender is now generally abhorrent to the conscience of the community."

Since when is the Supreme Court the Gallup Poll, to tell us what is or is not abhorrent to the conscience of the community? We hold elections to decide things like that. We send people to Congress, to state legislatures, or to the White House to make policy. Judges are appointed to tell us what is legal—not what they think the rest of us find "abhorrent."

As for Justice Stevens' notion that our views are "unambiguous" on this subject, they weren't unambiguous even to Justice Sandra Day O'Connor, who voted with him but wrote a separate opinion. And they certainly weren't "unambiguous" to dissenting Justice Antonin Scalia, who said that the evidence that this opinion represented the "views of our society" was "nonexistent."

Obviously, laws that authorize the execution of young murderers wouldn't be on the books in the first place if there were such widespread opposition to them as Justice Stevens' opinion implies. But there is a joker in his argument. What you and I and the rest of the peasants think is not what Justice Stevens is talking about. It is what he calls "leading members" of Western society believe that matters.

In other words, Justice Stevens is falling in line with what the morally self-anointed have made the vogue in fashionable circles—and he is doing so with just enough pretense of following the Constitution to insult the intelligence of everyone else.

The issue here goes well beyond the couple of dozen vicious young punks on death row, who have been saved by Justice Stevens' verbal sleight-of-hand. The deeper issue was clearly stated by Justice Antonin Scalia as whether we shall continue to have a tradition of "a government of laws and not of men."

Like all human ideals, that one has never been lived up to perfectly. But we don't abandon other ideals whenever someone violates them. If we did, we would be abandoning civilization to the barbarians among us.

A "government of laws and not of men" is radically different from a government where those in power simply issue whatever orders they feel like. Back in the days of the Roman Empire, the emperor could take another man's land, money, or wife, just because he felt like it. Such despotism was also common in other parts of the world, and remained so, long after Western civilization repudiated that concept.

It took centuries of struggle and bloodshed to establish the principle of a government of laws and not of men. But, over the past 35 years especially, the U.S. Supreme Court has been steadily moving us back in the opposite direction, with judges issuing more and more orders simply because they happen to feel one way rather than another.

Both the rule of law and the rule of "we the people" have been sacrificed to the presumptions of the morally arrogant. What we have been witnessing over the past generation has been nothing less than the slow but steady repeal of the American Revolution that we continue to celebrate each Fourth of July.

◆

WILL PROPERTY RIGHTS RETURN?

ONE OF THE REASONS for the food shortages in the former Soviet Union is that so much food spoils between the farm and the supermarket. It spoils because it does not belong to anybody. Those who handle it get paid the same salary, whether the food is carefully stored and preserved or not.

Property rights create vested interests in the preservation and improvement of a nation's resources. No species of animals that are owned is in any danger of extinction. Colonel Sanders is never going to let chickens become extinct. It is un-owned animals in the wild that are endangered, just as it is un-owned air and water that are polluted.

People who own no property at all benefit from property rights, because they benefit from living in an economy with a higher standard of living, made possible by having innumerable self-interested guardians of the economy's resources. In this sense, property rights are very similar to free speech rights, which do not exist just for the benefit of that one percent (or less) of the population who are writers or lecturers.

The whole political system would not operate as well if the government could silence its critics. Similarly, the whole economic system would not operate as well, if political control of resources replaced individual control. Both free speech rights and property rights belong legally to individuals, but their real function is social, to benefit vast numbers of people who do not themselves exercise these rights.

Russians who go hungry because of inadequate property rights in food production and distribution are not the only people who suffer from a society's neglect of property rights. Cities like New York, where rent control and housing codes can turn apartment buildings from assets into liabilities, have more than their share of homeless people sleeping outdoors in brutal winter weather while many apartment buildings are abandoned and boarded up.

Here too, the neglect of property rights has a major impact on people who themselves own no property.

The importance of property rights was better understood two centuries ago than it is today. The Constitution of the United States included property rights and contract rights among the basic rights protected in the first ten Amendments. Unfortunately, since the days of the New Deal, courts have tended to treat property rights as expendable, whenever they stand in the way of some political scheme for avowedly noble social goals.

The Fifth Amendment says that private property may not be taken for public purposes "without just compensation." But that provision of the Constitution has been circumvented in many ways, with many pious phrases about "the public interest," and courts have repeatedly allowed property rights to be violated under broad readings of the "commerce clause" of the Constitution or of the "police powers" of the government.

Now, at last, these trends are being seriously challenged, both intellectually and in the highest court in the land. The intellectual challenge has come from the "law and economics" movement, which began at the University of Chicago, and which is epitomized in Chicago law professor Richard Epstein's book, *Takings*. The legal challenge is now before the U. S. Supreme Court in cases involving people whose property has been devalued by various government regulatory schemes, without the "just compensation" required by the Constitution when property is taken.

When the government confiscates half your property—whether to build a military facility, a park, or a highway—it must compensate you. But when it destroys half the value of your property by zoning or environmental restrictions, courts have not required compensation, despite the economic equivalence of the two actions.

Yet government restrictions can take away any portion of the value of property, including more than 100 percent, when they turn an asset into a liability, as with many apartment buildings in New York City. The combination of costs entailed by housing codes and revenues restricted by rent control laws have turned many buildings into money-losing properties which no one would purchase, and whose current owners simply abandon, even at the risk of legal penalties for doing so.

Environmentalists, zoning advocates, and others have become alarmed at the prospect that the Supreme Court may reinstate property rights and require government agencies to compensate owners for destroying the value of their property. This would of course cramp the style of those who wish to impose all sorts of social schemes on others.

The merits of those schemes is not at issue. If they are worth the cost, then that cost should be paid. Current practices allow those costs to be hidden, as property rights disappear into thin air with a few magic phrases about "the public interest" or "police powers" or "the commerce clause."

Trading off costs against benefits is what an economy is all about. Property rights force a weighing of such trade-offs, instead of allowing local and federal agencies to impose high costs on others at no cost to themselves.

◆

COURT POLITICIANS

THE U.S. SUPREME COURT'S long-awaited decision on abortion—*Planned Parenthood vs. Casey*—is being subjected to all sorts of legal, political, sociological, and ideological analysis. However, its greatest significance may be in what it reveals about the continuing degeneration of one of the key institutions in the American system of government.

Whatever the merits or demerits of the Supreme Court's decision as social policy on abortion, its verbose, elusive, and self-contradictory reasoning is symptomatic of the kind of bad-faith arguments and actions that have undermined the public's faith in government in general, and demoralized their hopes for this country.

Ironically, the Court's decision refers to "institutional integrity" among the reasons given for its neither maintaining nor overturning the *Roe v. Wade* abortion decision of 1973, but instead rendering a decision that looks more like a political compromise than an application of legal principles. The last thing this country needs are nine more politicians, operating across the street from Congress.

Whether these judicial politicans carry labels like "liberal," "conservative," or "centrist" may be fascinating to the media, but not to anyone who thinks that judges should apply the written law. The issue is not whether someone is pro-choice or pro-life, but whether judges are on the bench to carry out the law or to impose their own social policy preferences under the guise of interpreting the Constitution.

Like so many 5 to 4 Supreme Court decisions, with fragmented partial concurrences providing shifting majorities for different parts of the decision, *Planned Parenthood vs. Casey* is long on rhetoric and short on legal principle. It speaks of "the right to define one's own concept of existence, of meaning, of the universe," and of "the wonder of creation."

When Supreme Court opinions begin to rhapsodize, it is a sure sign that the Justices are skating on very thin ice over very deep water. Although *Planned Parenthood vs. Casey* destroys much of *Roe vs. Wade*, the two cases are very much alike in being decided on the basis of notions created out of thin air to support Justices' social policy preferences. Both cases are worthy successors of the line of cases that began with Justice William O. Douglas basing his *Griswold vs. Connecticut* decision on "emanations" from the "penumbra" of legal principles.

The verbosity of these opinions is not unrelated to their lack of principle. You cannot get to the point if there is no point to get to. All you can do is to try to strike resonant chords—or, more bluntly, try to snow the public.

It would be no challenge at all to find ten Supreme Court decisions by Justice Oliver Wendell Holmes that would not add up to as many words as those in *Planned Parenthood v. Casey*. Holmes cut through the distractions to the legal principle involved. Today, many jurists flatter themselves that they are wrestling with the new complexities of modern life, when in fact they are struggling to extricate themselves from the labyrinth of their own inconsistencies.

Much space in the new abortion decision is expended trying to explain why the Supreme Court majority did not simply over-rule *Roe vs. Wade*, instead of gutting it and leaving the facade standing. Here it belabors the obvious, that legal precedent and the stability of the law are important—as if anyone had ever said otherwise. That rationale might be relevant if they were letting *Roe* stand, instead of pretending to let it stand.

One reason for giving great weight to legal precedents is that the people and the institutions of the country have made major commitments, based on the given legal framework, including court decisions.

Whatever the abstract merits or demerits of Supreme Court decisions, many generations past, which made possible the development of the whole monetary and financial superstructure of this country, overturning such a decision today would be catastrophic.

None of this applies to the abortion decisions that began with *Roe vs. Wade*. Every pregnancy begins and ends inside of one year. Whatever transitional adjustments must be made, they are still transitional.

The claim that the public is "relying" on the Delphic pronouncements of the Supreme Court on abortion, when even the Circuit Courts of Appeal cannot figure out what the Justices mean, is farcical.

Even the most beneficial principle can become disastrous as a fetish. The principle of upholding legal precedents is especially problematical in the wake of an era when judicial activism shattered innumerable earlier precedents.

To make all the recent activist decisions sacred as precedents is to abdicate Constitutional law to those reckless Justices like William Brennan and Harry Blackmun, who have made their own personal heartburnings "the law of the land."

◆

COURTING THE ANOINTED

ONE OF THE SCARIEST TALKS I have ever heard was given by a very sober and savvy man, Judge Laurence H. Silberman of the U. S. Circuit Court of Appeals in Washington. Judge Silberman's thesis was that his fellow judges seemed to him to be influenced by how their decisions would be perceived by the media and the intelligentsia.

Not long afterward, a Supreme Court decision came down in which the Justices themselves expressed concern about how their handling of the case would be seen by "the thoughtful part of the Nation."

Recently, Justice Anthony Kennedy gave a speech to the American Bar Association that was painfully embarrassing to watch, as he obviously tried to play up to them with current buzzwords. Just a few days ago, a friend of Justice David Souter was quoted as saying that Justice Souter sees his role as being "a healer of divisions in the country."

You might think that being a Justice of the Supreme Court would be a full-time job and a heavy enough responsibility that those on the Court would not have the time or the energy left to be looking out for their image or playing philosopher kings.

When millions of people, billions of dollars, and the future of freedom in the United States are affected by judicial decisions, why should federal judges be playing to the peanut gallery? With lifetime tenure and no one able to tinker with their paychecks, how much courage does it take for federal judges to uphold the law?

When men are sent into combat to put their young lives on the line for their country, is it too much to expect comfortable and insulated judges to carry out their duties without regard to their image or other personal vanities?

The media seem to be aware of their ability to influence some judges by the way they cover them. The *New York Times* lavished all sorts of praise on Justices Kennedy, Souter, and O'Connor in a long puff piece just before last year's abortion decision, in which those Justices were the crucial swing votes that kept *Roe v. Wade* from being openly reversed. Among other things, does this suggest that the impending decision was leaked?

Despite the bitter controversies that still rage over abortion, 20 years after *Roe v. Wade*, that decision was not just about abortion. More fundamentally, it was about the role of law itself.

Nothing written in the Constitution provided any basis for *Roe v. Wade*. The issue is not whether you are for or against abortion. The issue is whether judges should turn their courtrooms into places where the political agendas of the elite are enacted into law, when those agendas cannot be enacted into law by elected officials.

One of the favorite excuses for judicial policy-making is that courts were "forced" to act because legislatures "failed" to act. When the public does not want something done, it is not a failure when the legislature refuses to do it. That is called democracy.

When courts take over the job of imposing rejected elite doctrines on the masses—when it plays to the gallery of "the thoughtful part of the Nation"—then we have something very ugly, something that comes very close to a repeal of the American revolution, on the instalment plan.

Admittedly, those who wish to be honest judges and to uphold the law face a cruel dilemma. Decades of free-wheeling policy-making by the likes of Justices Harry Blackmun and William J. Brennan have left the legal landscape strewn with the wreckage of Supreme Court precedents without any genuine basis in the Constitution.

Both the Constitution and the precedents are things that a judge with honor and integrity would wish to uphold. However, the reckless judicial activism of the recent past has made that impossible.

When a choice must be made between upholding the Constitution and upholding these recent precedents, it cannot be easy. But what are Supreme Court justices there for, if not to make the tough calls?

What the much-celebrated "centrists" on the Supreme Court—Justices Anthony Kennedy, David Souter, and Sandra Day O'Connor— try to do is to work out some politic compromise, and then paper it over with pious rhetoric. The problem with that is not with the merits or demerits of their particular compromises, but that there is no principle left standing at the end of it all.

With no principle, there is no law. Anyone with power can issue orders, but arbitrary orders are not law, even when those orders come from judges. We may as well remove the words carved in stone over the entrance to the Supreme Court: "Equal Justice under Law."

"Take Your Chances with Evolving Standards" might be a more accurate motto today. While we are trying to explain to the Russians that a framework of known laws is essential for a free market and a free society, we have a Supreme Court that beclouds all sorts of issues with nebulous and inconsistent rulings—and even exalts this lack of principle into a principle in itself, "evolving standards."

Justices Antonin Scalia and Clarence Thomas, and Chief Justice William Rehnquist, have been more concerned about upholding the law as written, including both statutes and the Constitution, and less preoccupied with upholding all precedents at all cost. Mercifully, they have spared us any hand-wringing about what "the thoughtful part of the Nation" might say.

What Justices Kennedy, Souter, and O'Connor have in common is that they all came on the court tagged as "conservatives," supposedly meaning that they believed in carrying out the written law. But at crucial junctures, they have wavered and compromised with legal principles, thereby letting stand some liberal social policies which have no basis in the written law.

For that, they have been lionized in the media.

Cynics say that every man has his price, but you can at least have a higher price than that. Moreover, current media reactions are not the verdict of history.

◆

THE CONSTITUTION

"THE CONSTITUTION OF THE UNITED STATES is not a suicide pact," the late Supreme Court Justice Robert H. Jackson reminded his colleagues on the high bench.

The Constitution was made for a nation to survive under—not as a set of ideas to be stretched to the furthest extremes, without regard to the dangers this generates. Wise men created the Constitution. Clever men are destroying it, by reading it as a blank check for whatever adventures in social policy are in vogue among judges.

Those who wrote the Constitution and established a fledgling nation out of 13 recently independent colonies were well aware of the hazards of their undertaking—and proceeded with great caution as a result. In *The Federalist Papers* Alexander Hamilton, James Madison, and John Jay discussed the sad fates of other republics and democracies of earlier times, and struggled to prevent the same fate from overtaking the United States.

The Constitution avoided issues that would tear the country apart in its infancy—through silence in the case of slavery, through forbidding Congress to act, in the case of religion. The Constitutional convention of 1789 was not a seminar on moral philosophy, and the document that emerged from it was neither a manifesto nor a suicide pact. It was an attempt to create a nation that could endure, despite internal stresses and the external dangers of an international jungle, in which the United States was small and vulnerable.

Strong moral traditions underlay the Constitution, but they were implicit in its structure rather than explicit in ringing rhetoric. It had none of the flare and sweep of the Declaration of the Rights of Man, which accompanied the French Revolution of the same era.

But the French Revolution ended after one decade with the military despotism of Napoleon, while the U.S. Constitution not only endured but spread its freedom with the Thirteenth Amendment against slavery and the Fourteenth Amendment proclaiming equal rights under the law. The whole outlook on life, and the whole vision of man underlying it, were radically different as between the American Revolution and the French Revolution.

Many of the key figures behind the Constitution of the United States saw man's inherent limitations as severely restricting how much power anyone could be trusted with. It was this vision of human nature which produced the Constitution's elaborate scheme of checks and balances.

"It may be a reflection on human nature that such devices should be necessary to control the abuses of government," James Madison said. "But what is government itself but the greatest of all reflections on human nature?"

Alexander Hamilton likewise saw the only reason why government exists at all as the fact that "the passions of men will not conform to the dictates of reason and justice" unless forced to. He considered this to be as true of the elite as of the masses.

Without this crucial assumption about the inherent limitations of human beings, there would be no point in the Constitution's checks and balances, which prevent each branch of government from achieving unbridled power.

The French Revolution had no such assumption—and its leaders wielded the power of life and death "in the name of the people." It was the prototype of the revolutions which put their faith in the morally anointed. Its degeneration into despotism was also the prototype of the fate of such revolutions.

As the unbridled power of a succession of French revolutiuonary governments led to injustices, abuses, and chaotic and bloody policies, many regretted that the wrong people had gotten into power and had done many wrong things. They never saw the deeper problem, which was so clear to those who wrote the American Constitution—that no one could be trusted to wield the enormous power of government unchecked.

Ironically, as we approach the 200th anniversary of the Constitution, a whole generation of judges has increasingly abandoned the great principle behind it. That principle is a very limited role for government, with its restricted powers being exercised in the spirit of "a government of laws and not of men."

Too many judges today see themselves in the role of the morally anointed, issuing edicts to create "social justice," with the written law being over-ridden or "re-interpreted" out of existence when it stands in the way. Far from being guardians of the Constitution, these kinds of judges are engaged in the quiet repeal of the American Revolution, replacing it with the headier philosophy behind the French Revolution—the more ambitiously idealistic revolution, whose failure led to despotism.

There could be no better birthday present for the Constitution than an amendment ending life tenure for federal judges. They have shown in a thousand ways that they are not worthy of it and cannot be trusted with it— not if we want the Constitution to last another 200 years.

PART VII

THE RACIAL
SCENE

◆

"MINORITIES"

YEARS AGO, WHEN I WAS RUNNING A RESEARCH PROJECT in Washington, a memorandum came down from on high, telling us that there was money available to hire "minority" professionals for the summer, without having to take it out of the regular project budget.

"Wonderful!" I said. "There's a Jewish lady up at Princeton who wants to come down here and help me out, but I don't have any money to pay her."

This idea was shot down immediately.

"Jews are not a minority," I was told. "And Jews from Princeton are definitely not a minority."

It did no good to point out that Jews are only 3 percent of the population, and so must be a minority. Nor did it do any good to say that Jews were defined as an ethnic minority in the research project itself. The powers that be turned a deaf ear to all such arguments.

In a sense, they were right. The word "minority" had already become one of many politically corrupted words. It no longer meant a statistically smaller part of the population. It meant people you feel sorry for.

After all their achievements, nobody felt sorry for Jews any more. Therefore they were not a "minority."

Nobody feels sorry for Asian Americans anymore, after so many success stories. Therefore, they are increasingly excluded from "minority" status in programs and policies at some colleges and universities.

A few years ago, a memorandum from the U.S. Air Force Academy gave lower cut-off scores for "minority" applicants being recruited but Asian Americans had to meet the same standards as whites. Few institutions are so impolitic as to put such policies in writing or so unfortunate as to have them leak out. But there is growing evidence that this practice extends well beyond the Air Force Academy.

When Berkeley used verbal test score cut-offs to eliminate applicants in 1984 and 1986, "minority" students were exempted—but Asian American students were not. Many Asians were wiped out by the verbal cut-off scores because their strong suit tends to be math.

At Harvard, the test scores of Asian American applicants were virtually the same as those of white applicants, but the Asian Americans actually admitted had test scores substantially higher than those of whites who were admitted. In terms of test scores, Asians had to be better to get in.

It is not just Asians and Jews who lose their "minority" status because of outstanding performance. Some financial aid programs have also passed over those blacks who score above a certain level, in favor of those blacks who did poorly, who "really need" help. They want people they can feel sorry for.

Academic smoothies are never at a loss to explain away whatever they do. At M.I.T., for example, the director of admissions has responded to criticisms of large test score disparities among people admitted from different racial and sex backgrounds by downgrading the importance of test scores. Differences in test scores have only a modest correlation with later academic performance, he said.

This familiar argument is clever but phoney. The average M.I.T. student scores in the top one percent in math. Just where in that top one percent probably doesn't matter a lot, as the director of admissions says. But it does matter that he is in the top one percent.

By the same token, the difference of a few million dollars between one Rockefeller and another probably doesn't matter that much. But that doesn't mean that it makes no difference how much money you have.

It makes a very real difference that 90 percent of the white M.I.T. students score higher in math than the average black M.I.T. student. A substantially higher percentage of the black students fail to finish M.I.T., and those who do graduate have substantially lower grade-point averages.

The tragedy is that this waste— one-fourth of the black students don't graduate at M.I.I.—is completely unnecessary. The average black student at M.I.T. is well above the national average on math tests. He is just not in the stratospheric level of other M.I.T. students.

At most colleges, universities, or technical institutes, these same black students would be on the dean's list.

In short, black students with every prospect of success are artificially turned into failures by being mismatched with their college. This is not peculiar to M.I.T. It is a nationwide phenomenon among elite schools, who are more interested in having a good-looking body count from every group than they are in the price that has to be paid.

Everyone pays a very high price for this academic fad. Disadvantaged minority students pay the highest price of all. Asians may be lucky that they are not considered "minority."

◆

HISTORICAL APOLOGIES

AT THE TIME OF THE 50TH ANNIVERSARY of Japan's attack on Pearl Harbor, the Japanese parliament considered apologizing to the United States, but decided not to. Meanwhile, President Bush apologized to Japanese Americans for their internment during World War II. In 1992, Spain is supposed to apologize to the Jews who were expelled *en masse* from that country 500 years ago.

These collective apologies for historical actions taken by others may be seen as grand moral gestures by some, but in fact they exacerbate the already dangerous tendency to obliterate the crucial concept of personal responsibility. What possible meaning does it have, either logically or morally, for someone to apologize for what someone else did to a third party?

Are all people of Slavic ancestry to apologize to all Jews for the centuries of brutal anti-Semitism in Eastern Europe? And are all Jews to apologize to all Slavs for those Jewish slave-traders who, in earlier centuries, sold Slavs into bondage from Spain to the Ottoman Empire? What about all the atrocities of the Christians against the Moslems, or the Moslems against the Christians, during their centuries of warfare?

The list could go on and on. Historic wrongs can be found all over the globe. In fact, much of history consists of those wrongs. If all of us started apologizing to each other for all the wrongs of history, the noise would be deafening.

Many of those who emphasize the wrongs of history have a highly selective list of those wrongs, geared toward contemporary ideological politics. Thus, the wrongs of European imperialists against various Third World nations are to be kept alive as enduring grievances and—more to the point— enduring entitlements to largesse. However, the wrongs of any of these nations against each other, or against their own peoples, are passed over in silence, no matter how much worse they might have been.

Sometimes the argument is that we need to correct the contemporary effects of past wrongs. Seldom is any evidence either asked for or given to show that we know what those effects are. It is certainly not easy to know.

In many parts of the world, groups clearly mistreated historically have emerged better off educationally, economically, and socially than those who mistreated them. The Chinese minorities in various Southeast Asian countries have seldom had equal rights, but they have typically risen from initial poverty to a position where they are better off economically than the majority populations of Malaysia, Indonesia, or other countries in the region.

Much the same story could be told of immigrants from the Indian subcontinent who settled in East Africa or in Fiji, or of immigrants from Lebanon in West Africa, Italians in Argentina, and many others around the world. In a number of countries and a number of periods of history, it has been common for particular groups to take over substandard land left idle by others as "waste land"—and to become more successful farmers than others around them who were farming more fertile land.

We have barely scratched the surface in understanding why some groups prosper, even under bad conditions, or why others fail to utilize much better opportunities. Indeed, a whole tendentious vocabulary has arisen to obscure or bury such questions. Those who fail are said to have been "excluded" or denied "access." Those who succeed are said to have been "privileged." Again, evidence is neither asked nor given. This formula leaves out achievement—or even luck.

Would anyone (other than ideologues or intellectuals) say that Babe Ruth had more "opportunity" to hit home runs, when in fact he was the most walked batter in history?

This strange way of talking is not confined to a few fringe ideologues. It has caught on across the spectrum, and is now part of the mainstream mindset, at least among academics. Retired Harvard President Derek Bok, for example, said that to apply the same admissions standards to minority students as to others would be to "exclude them from the university." This was said more than a century after blacks began attending Harvard, entering and graduating without double standards during most of that time.

Much contemporary discussion of historic guilt is more than moral mushheadedness. Some of it is exploited quite skillfully by people whose careers depend on it. A whole class of "diversity consultants" or race relations specialists has come into existence to promote guilt among students, faculty and administrators at leading colleges and universities across the country.

At the University of Wisconsin, for example, an itinerant race relations specialist evoked "the repentant sobs of white students" at one of his workshops, which promoted the theme that virtually all whites were racists. Similar themes and similar techniques have been widely used from large universities like Harvard and Tulane to small colleges like Oberlin and Whitman.

Achieving justice in our own time is a task that taxes the resources of even the best societies. We should leave the past in the past.

◆

"AFFIRMATIVE ACTION" BACKLASH

"USUALLY I HAVE TO PULL TEETH to get my students to speak up in discussion sections, but I had no trouble at all in my American Government class last quarter on the day we discussed the Bakke decision. The anger in the room was quite palpable as each white (and Asian) student in each of my three sections chimed in to denounce affirmative action."

This letter from a woman who teaches at a well-known university points to a problem that is boiling at many colleges and universities, as well as in other American institutions—not to mention various other countries around the world. Black and Hispanic students in this lady's class defended affirmative action—except for one of the black students, who was academically outstanding and who said that affirmative action would stigmatize him as someone who came in "through the back door," even though he was in fact making it on his ability.

One of the reasons why it is hard to discuss many controversial issues sensibly is that people often do not bother to define what they are talking about. "Affirmative action" has meant many things in different times and places. In the beginning, it often meant simply a special effort to make sure that everybody received the same treatment, regardless of race, religion, or national origin. That is not what it usually means today.

Another early meaning for "affirmative action" was that special efforts needed to be made for disadvantaged groups, to bring knowledge of opportunities to them and to develop more skills among them, so that they could take advantage of these opportunities. Polls have shown that most Americans support such things, even though most Americans (including blacks and women) oppose preferential hiring.

Over the years, "affirmative action" has largely come to mean preferential policies—whether in employment, college admission, or elsewhere. This is what has polarized people, not only in the United States but also in India, Nigeria, Sri Lanka, New Zealand, and other countries.

These countries differ widely, as do the groups receiving the preferences. That makes it all the more remarkable that they share many similarities. The most common similarity is that preferences produce polarization. Where these preferential policies have gone on longer—in India and Sri Lanka, for example—the polarization has reached the stage of mob violence, bloodshed in the streets, and many innocent lives lost, often in hideous atrocities.

Are we in America heading in that direction? It is hard to know whether a growing number of ugly racial incidents adds up to a trend. Maybe we won't know until it is too late.

For a number of years now, many colleges have had racial harassment, confrontations and violence of a sort that they never had a generation ago. This is not a "vestige" of past racism, but a new backlash.

These incidents are not nearly as common on conservative campuses or in conservative areas such as the South. Indeed, liberal Massachusetts alone has more of these incidents than all the Southern states put together. Avant-garde institutions across the country—Berkeley, University of Massachusetts, Smith, Dartmouth—are where some of the ugliest racial polarization can be found.

A Ku Klux Klan leader was quoted recently as saying that affirmative action is one of his most effective talking points when recruiting whites for his racist organization. This and other such organizations are springing up in places far removed from their old stomping grounds and among educated people who would have had nothing to do with KKK, neo-Nazi, and other such movements before.

This does not mean that the college kids who oppose preferential treatment are about to put on white robes and start burning crosses. It does mean that we had better start to realize what is happening before things reach that point. Unfortunately, too many colleges across the country have simply tried to clamp the lid on tighter, so that expressing anger on such racial issues will be punished.

That is treating the symptom rather than the disease. But few colleges—or other institutions—are going to ask whether their own policies have contributed to the anger that has been building up.

Some see opposition to affirmative action as simply opposition to minority groups getting ahead by taking places that would otherwise go to whites. But, on some leading college campuses, Asians take far more places than blacks and Hispanics put together—and the Asians get praised for it. As an old song said: "It ain't what you do, it's the way that you do it."

There are many ways to help groups that need help. Preferential policies tend to produce a minimum of help and a maximum of backlash. Someone should do a study of a low-income ghetto or barrio to find out how many people there—if any—have actually benefitted from affirmative action.

Around the world, preferential policies tend to help the elite in the name of the masses. It is a great way for a professor, a lawyer, or a businessman to get special deals. But it does little or nothing for the truly disadvantaged individual—except make him more of a target for the backlash from the larger society.

◆

RACE AND RELIGION

CHRISTCHURCH, NEW ZEALAND: Is it necessary to go 10,000 miles away from the United States to have a rational discussion of race? Perhaps. Certainly it has been years since I have heard such a sober and thoughtful examination of racial and ethnic issues as during the meetings of the Mont Pelerin Society in New Zealand.

The Mont Pelerin Society is an international organization of free market supporters and its various conference meetings in New Zealand covered everything from foreign aid to philosophy. Among those on the panel discussing racial and ethnic issues, 3 out of 5 were American economists. Why couldn't we have met in the United States and had the same discussions at home?

Maybe we could have. But on most leading college and university campuses in the U.S., hoodlum behavior and storm trooper tactics would disrupt any public discussion of race or ethnicity that did not fit the prevailing dogmas. With 10,000 miles of ocean between ourselves and the intolerance of academia, it was possible to have a calm and candid discussion of issues that have become taboo at home.

One of the most thought-provoking talks was by Professor Jennifer Roback of George Mason University. She argued that the politicization of race was almost inevitable—and extremely dangerous. She noted the parallel with the politicization of religion, which caused so much death and destruction across the continent of Europe for centuries.

The First Amendment to the Constitution of the United States forbids Congress to pass any law respecting an establishment of religion. This essentially took religion off the political agenda, precisely in order to avoid the traumas that Europe had gone through. Professor Roback suggested that a similar amendment was needed to take race off the political agenda.

Many who are convinced that government policies have greatly benefitted disadvantaged racial minorities would no doubt be horrified by any such suggestion. However, the most important benefit the federal government has conferred on racial minorities over the past half century has been destroying state government discrimination in the South. Had race been off-limits to the politicians, there would have been no Jim Crow laws in the first place. Neither would the law have recognized the enslavement of one race by another.

Particular policies such as "affirmative action" have helped particular individuals or classes—usually those individuals and classes who were already more fortunate to begin with. But the less educated and poorer blacks have fallen further behind during the era of "affirmative action." This pattern of advancement for the elite and retrogression for the masses under such policies is not peculiar to blacks or even to the United States.

The closer you look at the actual consequences of government policies on race and ethnicity, in countries around the world, the more depressing the picture becomes. It is not just that these policies have not worked, or have been economically counterproductive. The politicization of race and ethnicity has escalated hostility and violence between groups in country after country.

The current situation is strikingly parallel to the slaughters that grew out of politicizing religious differences in times past. Whether with race or religion, it is not the differences as such that produce the animosity and violence. All sorts of groups have co-existed peacefully for generations, until some demagogue came along to whip up their emotions against each other— or until some government programs gave them freebies to fight over.

The great religious battles that tore countries apart were not just over ideas and beliefs. Money and power were at stake—including the power to persecute other religions. If you were a Catholic in Ireland two centuries ago, you still had to pay taxes to the established Protestant church and you couldn't sit in Parliament or do all sorts of other things that Protestants were permitted to do.

Buddhists and Hindus co-existed peacefully for generations in colonial Ceylon. But once it became an independent nation (now called Sri Lanka), the government created privileges for the Buddhist Sinhalese majority. Group polarization soon reached the point of riots, atrocities, and civil war.

The United States already has the kind of Constitutional Amendment Professor Roback suggested. It is the Fourteenth Amendment that mandates "equal protection" for all people. Unfortunately, clever judges twisted its interpretation in the nineteenth century to allow racial discrimination, and have twisted it more recently to allow racial and ethnic preferences.

The worst racial and ethnic polarization in any American institutions are today found in our leading colleges and universities, where all sorts of double standards prevail and all sorts of benefits are earmarked for particular racial and ethnic groups. As resentments against these groups increase and erupt in ugly incidents, the response has been to create still more racially earmarked benefits.

It defies both logic and history to respond to polarization with more of the things that create polarization. We can only hope that this pattern does not spread from the campuses to American society in general.

◆

APARTHEID IN ADOPTIONS

ONE OF THE LEAST REPORTED FORMS of child abuse are official policies that keep orphans from being adopted because of arbitrary dogmas by ideological zealots.

Many children are kept in limbo for years, either in institutional care or being shunted from one foster home to another, because the people who wish to adopt them are not of the same race as the child. The policies, regulations, or statutes that mandate such *apartheid* are not products of the Ku Klux Klan, neo-Nazis, or other such groups, but instead originate with people on the other end of the political spectrum—people for whom being "politically correct" is more important than letting a child have a home.

Not only are orphans kept orphans; some children who have been raised from infancy by people of another race have been forcibly taken away from the only parents they have ever known. The sight of both parents and children breaking down into heart-broken sobs in the courtroom has left the zealots and the bureaucrats unmoved.

In one case, an American Indian girl who had been raised from infancy to adolescence by a white couple was taken away to an Indian reservation she had never seen before—a place where she was treated as an outcast by the strangers around her.

Currently, in San Francisco, only a temporary restraining order is preventing the Department of Social Services from snatching a one-year old black child from the only home she has ever known—the home of a white couple who took in her when she was 5 days old and a crack baby.

"You are not ethnically or racially matched with this child," the Department of Social Services wrote. "It is not appropriate for you to adopt her."

Apparently it is "appropriate" to break a child's heart and cast her out into the world, to spend her life in an orphanage or wandering like a little vagabond from one foster home to another, perhaps for years on end.

These are not isolated events. A San Francisco attorney specializing in such cases says that she gets "calls all the time from parents telling me horror stories about DSS ripping kids out of their homes"—not because the children have been mistreated, but for the opposite reason: Temporary foster parents have become so attached to the child that they now want to adopt.

Such situations and such inhuman policies are not peculiar to San Francisco. They are nationwide.

Minnesota, for example, has its "Minority Heritage Preservation Act" to enforce apartheid in adoption. This act explicitly prohibits the courts from deciding such cases solely on the basis of what is best for the child.

If there were ample numbers of black couples waiting to adopt black children, then a preference for such couples over white couples might well be understandable. But no such choice exists.

A disproportionate share of the orphans are minority, and a disproportionate share of the couples seeking to adopt are white. That is why the prospect of transracial adoptions arises in the first place.

Those who promote and defend apartheid adoption policies speak loftily of "the essentiality of a minority family in transmitting minority values," and the "societal value of group self-determination." The National Association of Black Social Workers says that black children should be placed only with black families, so that they can receive "the total sense of themselves."

Such puffed-up rhetoric has become more important than children's lives, at least to the grievance-mongers with separatist ideologies. Moreover, so-called "responsible" officials across the country have caved in to these strident loudmouths, who are more concerned with their own dogmas and their own turf than with the fate of flesh-and-blood human beings.

Those who oppose adoptions across racial lines are long on words and short on evidence, as they conjure up imaginary traumas for the adopted children. But where serious scholarly studies have been done on black children raised by white families, these bogeymen are not found

Whether measured by I.Q., self-esteem, or other criteria, these children compare well with children of any color, raised by people of any color. This is hardly surprising. Minority children are not likely to be adopted by the Archie Bunkers of the world, but by more enlightened people.

What does a prissy, bureaucratic word like "appropriate" mean, when weighed against shattering a child's life? Even if, by some miracle, the little toddler in San Francisco should find another couple equally devoted to her, will she ever feel secure again, after having been snatched away from her home before, for reasons that no one-year-old could understand?

Indeed there are no real reasons that anyone of any age should accept or tolerate. There are only shallow and cheap dogmas by those mean-spirited enough to sacrifice helpless children to their own petty vanity.

◆

STEREOTYPES VERSUS THE MARKET

THERE IS MUCH LOOSE TALK about "stereotypes" these days. Often, it makes me think back to an episode many years ago.

Back during the Korean war, a young Marine named Albert Greuner graduated from the photography school at Pensacola Naval Air Station and was ordered to report for duty as a photographer at the photo lab at Camp Lejeune, North Carolina. Yet, when he arrived at Camp Lejeune, he discovered that his orders had been changed. He was now told to report instead to the supply depot, where he was assigned to handle photographic supplies.

Baffled and disappointed by the sudden change, Greuner told me his story—and was further taken aback when I burst out laughing. In reality, I was part of the reason for his misfortune.

Some months earlier, the photo lab received its first group of graduates from the photography school at Pensacola. By and large, we were better photographers than those they had. However, we were also young draftees with attitudes wholly different from those of career Marines.

We saw the Marine Corps as just an unwelcome interlude in our lives, and we were less than awed by our superiors or by their rules or orders. We hung out together and became known—not always affectionately—as "the Pensacola gang."

When the captain in charge of the photo lab had about as much of us as he could stand, he cleaned out the lot of us, breaking up the Pensacola gang and scattering us individually to various other places around the base. When he later received word that another photographer from Pensacola had been assigned to his lab, the captain had him transferred, sight unseen.

It so happened that Greuner was a different sort of fellow, and would probably have gotten along very well in the photo lab. But he never got the chance—because of the behavior of his predecessors.

Today, that would be called "stereotyping" and the captain would be criticized for not judging Greuner as an individual. However, whatever the merits of that argument in this particular case, no one goes around judging everyone as an individual, however popular such cant may be.

When you are walking down a dark street at night and see a shadowy figure in an alley up ahead, do you judge him as an individual—or do you cross the street and pass on the opposite side? Judging him as an individual could cost you your life. It may turn out that he is just a kindly neighbor out walking his dog, but you discover that only after the fact.

The high cost of knowledge is often overlooked when discussing social policies, and especially social policies in the emotionally charged area of race and ethnicity. In real life, decisions are based on imperfect knowledge, simply because there is no other kind.

Recently a black, middle class professional wrote of his resentment when he was asked to pay for his meal in advance in an Asian-owned restaurant— especially after he noted that a white couple that came in was not asked to do the same. Was this arbitrary racism or self-protection based on experience in this neighborhood? That was the key question he did not ask—nor do most journalistic stories or even scholarly studies.

The same man also expressed resentment at the looks of aversion he received from fellow blacks in another establishment, because he was wearing his hair in dreadlocks. Clearly this was not a question of racism, but of repugnance toward the kind of people who "make a statement" with that kind of hairstyle.

Apparently, neither blacks, whites, nor Asians judge each person as an individual. Probably no one else in the world does either, though the intelligentsia may talk that way.

Fortunately, the marketplace puts a price on incorrect generalizations, as it does on all sorts of other incorrect assumptions behind economic decisions. Even the most racist owner of a professional basketball team could not refuse to hire blacks, unless he were willing to face bankruptcy—and thereby cease to be a basketball owner.

Theoretically, racists could simply absorb the losses created by their own discrimination. Empirically, it is very hard to find people who are willing to lose hard cash, in order to discriminate. Racists may prefer their own group to others, but they prefer themselves most of all.

That is why discrimination has always been most prevalent where it costs discriminators the least—in government employment, in regulated utilities, or in non-profit organizations. That was true throughout the pre–civil rights era, just as reverse discrimination is generally strongest in such organizations today.

This is not an American pattern but a world-wide pattern. Yet those who wish to fight against discrimination often try to move employment decisions and other decisions out of the marketplace and into the hands of people who pay no price—politicians, bureaucrats, and judges.

◆

A LOOK BACK

MY CHILDHOOD DID NOT INCLUDE many material things that most people who live in poverty have today. But I did not grow up carrying the burden of being "poor."

We had everything that most of the people in our neighborhood had. In the early years down South, that seldom included frills like electricity or hot running water. But there were no deep-thinkers whimpering over us and no psychologists or social workers to call every rough spot in our lives a "trauma." We wouldn't have known what they were talking about if they had.

Since this was Charlotte, North Carolina in the 1930s, when the kids from our all-black neighborhood went to school, it was an all-black school. Decades later, a Supreme Court decision would say that the psychological burden of being separated from whites would impair out ability to learn, so that our education was unequal—and therefore unconstitutional.

Make no mistake about it, our education was unequal. But that wasn't the reason. I cannot recall anyone who gave a moment's attention to the fact that there were no white kids in our schools. There were no white people in our churches, our homes, or our barbershops. If we had found white kids in our schools, we would have wondered what was going on.

Just how inferior the education was became painfully clear when we moved north and I went to school in Harlem. Everyone else in the class was miles ahead of me. It was still a black school, though. The difference was that these kids had had better education.

Eventually, I went to racially integrated schools in New York. But this was after I had caught up educationally. The transition was not nearly as hard as the transition from the Charlotte school to the Harlem school.

Down South, everybody was either black or white, and that was it. Now I discovered that there were all kinds of different brands of white people. Some called themselves Jews, others Irish, still others Italians, and some German, Greek, or Armenian. It seemed like a needless complication and nuisance to me at the time.

People of today find it hard to conceive of what it was like in those days—or even to believe it when you tell them. A young New Yorker recently shuddered visibly when I mentioned the park in Harlem where I took my dog for a walk as a kid. Nobody in his right mind would do that today in that park.

The great untold story of black people in America is the level of decency, community, and personal pride developed long ago under the most adverse conditions. The level of unwed motherhood among black women in 1920 was less than one-fourth of what it is today—and slightly lower than that among white women today.

It was nothing unusual for whites to go to nightclubs in Harlem, or to baseball games in the Polo Grounds or to attend City College there. Milton Friedman's wife once mentioned that she and Milton used to go dancing at the Savoy Ballroom in Harlem—as did other white couples at that time.

When things turned bad in Harlem—and in other ghettoes across the country—whites could simply stay away. It was the blacks who remained and suffered as crime rates soared, education deteriorated, and the decay of buildings was matched by the decay of people and the fragmentation of families.

Few seem to notice that these tragedies coincided with a social deterioration in white America, as the fashionable new ideas of the 1960s spread across the media, the political arena, the campuses and the courtrooms.

Blacks, as a vulnerable group trying to catch up, were more hard hit than most as social tinkering ruined one institution after another, and undermined behavioral restraints at all social levels. The murder rate among blacks was actually declining for years— before the sweeping legal reforms of the 1960s were followed by skyrocketing murder rates among blacks and whites alike. More black males passed the tough entrance examination to New York's Stuyvesant High School in 1938 than in 1984, even though the black population of New York was much smaller in 1938.

Looking back, it is easy to see now that I was very lucky to be born when I was—which meant being educated at a time when ghetto schools were still capable of educating, and reaching adulthood just as the old system of racial discrimination was crumbling, and before the new deep thinking created a whole range of new tragedies.

No one can go back, even if he wanted to. But we can go forward with a more sober understanding of what contributes to progress and what has simply undermined existing achievements and existing decency. Too often we abandoned what worked in favor of what sounded good—as explained by "experts."

◆

THE UN-QUOTA

THERE ARE VERY FEW WORDS you can't use in public today. However, "quota" is one of these few. In polite society, the proper euphemisms are "goals," "diversity" or "equal opportunity."

When University of Michigan President James Duderstadt was asked about admissions quotas for minority students, he replied: "There is no quota system at the U-M." In fact, he said, "We've never had quotas." However, he also added: "We seek a student body composition that is reflective of the national composition."

Doesn't that sound more high-toned? Lawyers have long referred to this kind of reasoning as "a distinction without a difference." But no one expects logic from a college president.

A recent newsletter of the American Historical Association featured "Guidelines for Hiring Women Historians in Academia." Off-hand, you might think that hiring a female historian was not very different from hiring a male historian. And in fact the American Historical Association newsletter never really got around to explaining the difference.

Instead, the AHA listed all kinds of statistics on women historians and suggested the "proportion of tenure appointments that should go to women to achieve equity." But quotas? Never.

There was a time when civil rights meant civil rights—and when there was a long struggle to get them. Today those are just two words put into the title of legislation to scare Congressmen out of voting against it. Last year, this tactic helped get the so-called Civil Rights Restoration Act passed by Congress.

President Bush wisely vetoed that bill, which would have brought quotas out of the closet and made them the law of the land—though without using the Q-word itself. This year, that bill is back again, like a movie sequel. Like most sequels, it is no improvement on the original.

Intellectuals and politicians may be hung up on words but the public is more interested in realities. Polls increasingly show public resistance to preferential treatment, regardless of what it is called.

What makes a bill a quota bill is not what label it uses but whether it defines employment discrimination through statistics. If employers can be dragged into court because of the racial body count among their employees, then they are going to save themselves mega-bucks in legal bills by hiring through quotas. There is nothing mysterious about any of this.

One of the U.S. Supreme Court decisions that set off this latest political crusade for "restoring" the new version of "civil rights" involved the Wards Cove Packing Co., a Seattle firm which operates a cannery up in Alaska during the salmon season. It is well worth scrutinizing this case to see what the words "civil rights" have come to mean—and to see what hassles an employer can be put through on a purely statistical basis.

Back in November 1973, racial discrimination charges were filed with the Equal Employment Opportunity Commission, against the Wards Cove Packing Co. After nearly a decade, every single claim of discrimination was shot down in a federal district court ruling in October 1983.

After a detailed, 73-page examination of all the allegations of discrimination, the trial judge ruled that Wards Cove had "not discriminated on the basis of race," whether in hiring, firing, promoting, paying, housing, or feeding its employees. "Similarly situated applicants are treated equally," the judge said.

You might think that would be the end of it. But you would be wrong. After nearly four more years in litigation, the Ninth Circuit Court of Appeals in September 1987 over-ruled the trial court—largely on statistical grounds. The trial court had not applied "disparate impact analysis" in which claims can be "proved through statistical evidence."

From there, it was on to the Supreme Court. In June 1989, the high court ruled that the trial judge should take a look at racial statistics but that statistics alone were not enough to have someone presumed guilty of discrimination. The Supreme Court's refusal to worship at the shrine of statistics was what set off loud outcries of "a setback for civil rights" and the new legislation in Congress.

In January 1991, after examining racial statistics, the same trial judge made the same ruling as before, on charges that originated with the EEOC 17 years earlier. Once again, the charges didn't stand up.

Given the high cost of lawyers, all this back and forth between courts, for all these years, cannot be cheap. Obviously, many employers will find it cheaper to hire by quotas if "disparate impact" statistics are made decisive again in the name of "civil rights."

They won't call it a quota of course. There are all sorts of euphemisms already available.

-- ◆ --

"LEADERS" AND "SPOKESMEN"

TELEVISION AND NEWSPAPERS are constantly telling us what women want, what blacks want, what the elderly want, or what some other group wants. Usually this means what some organized noisemakers want. These noise-makers may be called "leaders" or "spokesmen" by the media but often their views have no relationship to the views of the groups in whose name they speak.

During controversies over whether English should be the official language, and whether it should be the language in which Asians, Hispanics and others are taught in school, all sorts of bitter complaints have come from "leaders" and "spokesmen" for various non-English-speaking minorities. The controversies have been especially bitter in California, where there are many immigrants whose native language is not English.

A recent poll among Filipinos, Hispanics, and Chinese in and around San Francisco showed that their views on language were radically different from the views of their "leaders" and "spokesmen." More than two-thirds of all the Hispanics polled approved of making English the official state language. So did more than three fourths of the Chinese and 90 percent of the Filipinos.

This was especially striking because more than a third of these Hispanics did not speak English in their own homes. Neither did nearly half of the Filipinos and more than half of the Chinese. As one Hispanic man put it, "If we do not learn English, we will never get ahead."

In addition, despite bitter complaints by "leaders" and "spokesmen" for such groups that they are treated unfairly by immigration officials or border officials, 86 percent of the Hispanics denied that they or any member of their families had ever been treated unfairly by these officials. So did 91 percent of the Chinese and 92 percent of the Filipinos.

College and university campuses across the country are full of student "leaders" and "spokesmen" for various minority groups. Academic administrators are quick to cave in to demands made in the name of these groups, without the slightest attempt to find out whether the views of minority students themselves coincide with the views of the noisemakers.

Last summer a group of Hispanic students at Stanford sent a letter to the university president, saying that the local Hispanic establishment did not speak for them and in fact engaged in harassment of Hispanic students who opposed the militant party line. After the local establishment denied harassment, a representative of other Hispanic students again complained of "strongarm tactics" and pointed out that only 15 percent of Hispanic students at Stanford had ever participated in any of the activities of the group that speaks so boldly in their name.

Noisemakers acting as self-appointed "leaders" and "spokesmen" for other ethnic groups, for women, and for others have been kow-towed to by academic administrators on many campuses across the country. College deans and presidents routinely accept what noisemakers say and demand as the authentic voice of whatever group they claim to represent. Sometimes this is naivete but often it represents a pragmatic judgment that the noisemakers are organized and can easily become troublemakers, whether or not they speak for anybody besides themselves.

It is not at all uncommon for noisemakers to intimidate members of the very group for whom they claim to be speaking. This intimidation may be physical or social. For example, a black South African student who came to America to escape apartheid discovered a new apartheid being imposed by black campus militants. "I and a few other black students were labeled Uncle Toms for sitting with whites in the cafeteria," said Mark Mathabane, author of the book *Kaffir Boy*.

James Meredith, who braved racism and dangers to his life to become the first black student at the University of Mississippi in 1962, was in 1988 kept off the campus of Hollins College by the Black Student Alliance there. The BSA had originally invited Meredith to speak at Hollins but the invitation was cancelled after they learned of what he had said at nearby William & Mary College. He had supported family values and hard work, including hard work in college.

Widespread media acceptance of noisemakers as "leaders" and "spokesmen" gives them a leverage out of all proportion to their numbers—and a leverage dangerous to all groups in this society. A vocal fringe can generate enormous hostility between groups, even if most of the people in each group have common sense, decency, and good will. What most people think is not what is featured in the media.

When the media feature outrageous accusations, demands, threats and disruptions by a vocal fringe—and depict that fringe as representative of the group—such distortion can only contribute to a growing polarization.

———————————————— ◆ ————————————————

GRATITUDE TO FAT CATS

IN A RECENT TELEVISION DISCUSSION of racial issues, one of the fat cats in the Washington black establishment attributed the economic advancement of blacks to the civil rights marches, in which he participated a quarter of a century ago. The suggestion was that those blacks who disagree with him today are ungrateful.

There is something a little obscene about people with six-figure salaries suggesting that other blacks owe them something. These black "leaders" and "spokesmen" have already parlayed race into big bucks, political perks, and media visibility for themselves. What do people in the ghetto owe them?

There is also a question of historical accuracy. The Big Lie that has been repeated for a generation now is that black Americans owe their economic progress to the civil rights movement in general or to "affirmative action" in particular. The blatant self-interest of those who are promoting this line never seems to be noticed by the media.

No one denies the civil rights movement a share of the credit for having advanced civil rights. But the economic advancement of blacks, both absolutely and relative to whites, began long before the civil rights movement of the 1960s, and was due to the individual efforts of millions of black people trying to better their own lives.

Hard statistics show that this advancement did not begin in the 1960s, was not even accelerated during the 1960s—and actually began to stall during the 1970s, when "affirmative action" started. Affirmative action has produced benefits for the elite, but that is not where the real problem is.

Even on the civil rights front, such landmark legislation as the Civil Rights Act of 1964 was a national response to racial issues, led by a man with few black voters among his constituents—Senator Hubert Humphrey of Minnesota. Let's not airbrush out of the picture everyone except the racial "spokesmen" who came to do good and stayed to do well.

Civil rights are important, in and of themselves, but they are no magic ingredient for economic and social progress. The Utopian expectations that they would be were doomed to disappointment from the outset. Some of us said so, even during the heyday of the civil rights movement back in the 1960s, though our voices were drowned out in the chorus of self-congratulation by our "leaders."

Like so many people with only one string to their bow, these "leaders" saw the economic disappointments which followed the civil rights revolution as a sign that civil rights had just not been pushed far enough. Their skills and talents were all specialized toward lobbying white people, not developing the potentialities of black people.

Any realistic assessment of the effects of the civil rights establishment on blacks and other minorities over the past generation cannot limit itself to their positive effects, important as these positive effects may be. The minority elite establishment, now solidly entrenched within the Washington beltway, has been part of a larger coalition which has pushed a much broader political agenda.

That broader agenda has included everything from an expansion of criminals' "rights" to environmental extremism and support of teachers' unions that have made public schools immune to any demands for decent education. Have minorities gained or lost, on net balance, from such an agenda?

Minority "leaders" who went along with these political deals have no incentive to go back and add up all the pluses and minuses for minority communities. On the contrary, they have every incentive—psychic as well as political—to go on believing that they have been doing a great job. Any negative consequences too blatant to be ignored can always be blamed on their all-purpose explanation, racism.

By going along with the broader agenda of the political left, the civil rights establishment shares responsibility for the dramatic upward spiral of criminality which began in the 1960s, as punishment became less and less likely. No one has been hurt more by this rising crime rate than minority communities, ravaged by violence on an unprecedented scale.

Other nostrums of the political left have destroyed housing and jobs, and undermined education and the family itself. Minority communities have been harder hit than anyone else by all these negative developments as well.

If the fat cats of the civil rights establishment want to take credit for all the achievements of other blacks, then let them also take "credit" for all this destruction which they have helped their white liberal allies unleash.

As more and more blacks become disenchanted with their media-anointed "leaders," these critics are routinely accused of ingratitude for all that the well-heeled black elite have done for them. At the very least, we need to look at the whole picture before deciding how much gratitude they are owed—if any.

◆

RACIAL STATISTICS

RACIAL STATISTICS HAVE BECOME AN INDUSTRY—if not a hustle. Typical of these statistics was a recent study by the Federal Reserve Board, showing that black applicants for mortgage loans are turned down 34 percent of the time, compared to 14 percent for white applicants.

To the media, and sometimes even to courts of law, statistical differences are the same thing as discrimination. Buried in a newspaper account of this study is mention of some "limitations" of the study, namely that "it didn't take into account the applicants' credit histories or the level of their existing debt."

These are two of the most important factors in determining whether or how much to lend to whom. Another major factor is the net worth of the credit applicant. Blacks average less net worth than whites in the same income brackets. In a census study published last year, even blacks in the highest income bracket averaged slightly lower net worth than whites in the second highest income bracket.

Given the history of the United States, and how recently even affluent blacks have achieved that status, it is hardly surprising that they have not accumulated as much in assets as whites who have been affluent for generations and have inherited assets from parents or grandparents.

Blacks and whites differ along many dimensions, just as all sorts of other groups differ along many dimensions in countries around the world. Despite the widespread assumption that statistical disparities between groups are strange and sinister, they are in fact commonplace all over this planet.

In the media, however, these mundane realities are ignored in favor of racial hype. Unfortunately, the chief victims of that hype are likely to be blacks, and especially young blacks.

How are you going to tell a young black man to work hard, or study hard, in order to get ahead, when both the media and many so-called "leaders" are constantly telling him that everything is rigged against him? Why knock yourself out on the job, or miss the Saturday night party in order to study, if whitey is just waiting in ambush to pull the rug out from under you anyway?

There have always been racists, but there has not always been racial hype on the scale that we are seeing today. Generations of blacks have shown that racists can be overcome, but we have yet to find out if debilitating hype can be overcome. So far, it doesn't look good.

One of the most painful social phenomena of our time is the deliberate refusal of many black students to work up to their capacity. We are not talking about laziness. We are talking about deliberately refusing to achieve, about stigmatizing those black students who do their best as "trying to act white."

Crazy? Not if you believe the racial hype. Why be a chump and play the man's game, if everything has been so rigged that you can't really get anywhere anyway? At least keep your self-respect by letting him know that he can shove it.

Schools across the country are reporting this attitude among black students. The pressure against those youngsters who do their work and try to master their subjects can be overwhelming, whether it takes the form of social ostracism or physical violence. We are watching a whole generation destroying its future.

Even some black leaders and white liberals have begun to notice this dangerous situation and to be alarmed about it. Few of them, however, are willing to take responsibility for their own role in creating the atmosphere behind such self-destructive attitudes.

They were addressing policy-makers or white society when they paraded their statistics and made their political pitches. Apparently it never occurred to them that others were listening—and drawing the logical inferences.

This steady drumbeat of racial hype and paranoia has long since reached the point of diminishing returns, as far as gaining more government benefits or other concessions from the white population. There is a reason why Democratic politicians are keeping their distance from racial issues during election years.

Only two large groups of people are affected by the continuation of racial hype. Just as super-patriotism is the last refuge of a scoundrel, super-identity is the last refuge of the hustler. Some make a career out of it and others try to escape blame for their own incompetence or criminal behavior—former Mayor Marion Berry of Washington being a classic example—by blaming their troubles on racism.

The other large group affected by racial paranoia are the next generation of blacks—those on whom all the hopes of the race's future depend. Is it worth it to sacrifice them, for the benefit of a handful of hustlers?

◆

MORAL MONOPOLY

ONE OF THE SAD PATTERNS OF HISTORY is the evolution of idealistic movements into corrupt or tyrannical institutions.

With all the horrors and bloodshed inflicted on many countries around
the world by Communism, it began as a movement with humanitarian aims.
Many people all over the world sacrificed their own interests, and even risked
their lives, to try to create a better world through the Communist movement.
Yet this tyranny slaughtered more people than died in Hitler's Holocaust.

On a smaller scale and in milder forms, all sorts of other insurgent
movements have eventually reached the point of becoming counterproductive and betraying the ideals with which they started. Regulatory reforms,
intended to protect the public from monopolies, have repeatedly evolved
into government-sponsored cartels that exploited the consumer worse than
ever.

The sad fact is that the civil rights movement, after its great achievements
of the 1950s and 1960s, has not only begun to fizzle out but has even evolved
into an institution and a class serving only their own interests, both financial
and ideological.

Few things are more destructive to the minority communities, in whose
name they speak, than crime, unemployment, and an educational system so
appalling that hopes of a better life are snuffed out early for youngsters in
the ghettoes and barrios across the country. Yet civil rights organizations have
dutifully lined up behind their liberal political allies and financial benefactors,
whose policies have made all these problems worse over the past generation.

Although the civil rights establishment owes its clout to its self-pro-
claimed role as "spokesman" for minority communities, what it actually says
is often at the opposite pole from the beliefs expressed by minority peoples
themselves. Blacks, for example, are in favor of school choice or voucher
plans by an even larger majority than among whites, but the civil rights
establishment lined up with its labor union allies and benefactors in opposition to anything that would threaten the public school monopoly and the
power of the teachers' unions.

Cynical deal-making is nothing new inside the Washington beltway, but
the media image of civil rights "leaders" remains that of spokesmen for the
interests of minorities. Only slowly has it begun to dawn on some in the
media that there is a growing gap between what the civil rights establishment

says and the views expressed by minority people themselves in poll after poll.

Nowhere was this gap more blatant than during the Senate confirmation hearings for Judge Clarence Thomas. Civil rights big shots came out against him but blacks as a whole supported Judge Thomas by an even larger majority than among whites.

The elevation of Clarence Thomas to the Supreme Court may well be an historic turning point in the history of the civil rights establishment. The fraudulence of its claim to speak for blacks was exposed, and its political clout was defied successfully.

Justice Thomas broke a political barrier and a taboo—and that will no doubt make it harder for the old-line civil rights big shots to intimidate other blacks into falling in line or remaining silent. For the black community as a whole, it can only be a benefit to be able to hear many voices before deciding what approaches and policies are more promising for the advancement of a people.

Those who see political power begin to slip from their hands, and who are losing the moral monopoly they once claimed, are not taking it gracefully. They are lashing out bitterly, wildly, and desperately, with every kind of cheap shot and character assassination.

Anita Hill was one symptom of this. Federal Judge Leon Higginbotham has become another, with a long, ugly, and cheap public denunciation of Justice Thomas.

Higginbotham drags in everything from Clarence Thomas' interracial marriage to his "ambition," offers him a gratuitous lecture on the abortion issue, and questions whether he was a "competent" choice for the Supreme Court.

It is hard to imagine what Higginbotham hoped to accomplish with this diatribe, other than a venting of his spleen. Surely, if Clarence Thomas was not intimidated by the Senate Judiciary Committee, he is not going to be worried about some judge two layers down from him—especially not one who makes a jerk of himself in public.

Maybe it is hard to be stuck on the same district court for 20 years, while others are elevated to higher appellate courts. More than that is involved, however. The sense of a moral monopoly, which runs through the statements of Higginbotham and others, is one no longer so widely accepted as in the past.

There are still some white liberals who can be cowed into silence by the kind of moral intimidation that Higginbotham tries to practice, but there are increasing numbers of young blacks and young whites alike who will not be scared out of thinking for themselves.

What we are seeing is a changing of the guard. And the old guard will not go quietly.

◆

RACIAL PARANOIA

OF ALL THE QUESTIONS I have heard from audiences, during 25 years of giving lectures, one question stands out more than any other. It was asked by an earnest young black student at Marquette University.

"Even though I am about to graduate from Marquette," he said, "what *hope* is there for me?"

The question hit like a body blow. There was probably twice as much opportunity for this young man as there was for his father, and ten times as much as for his grandfather.

But somebody had gotten to his mind—and that would be a heavy handicap for him to carry out into the world. Why would anybody put such a burden on the next generation of minority young people?

Racial paranoia is being actively promoted by many people for many purposes. Some want nothing more than notoriety and whatever following, influence, and money that brings. Others find racial paranoia useful politically, not only to get votes but also as a refuge when their own incompetence or criminality are exposed.

Bush-league messiahs and corrupt politicians are nothing new. What is new—and disturbing—is their growing support from mainstream, "respectable" minority leaders and organizations. When Benjamin Hooks of the NAACP lent credence to Washington Mayor Marion Barry's claim that his prosecution on drug charges was racial persecution, this was one of the signs of the times—one of the bad signs.

It used to be said that patriotism was the last refuge of a scoundrel. Today, group patriotism or racial paranoia provides that refuge for many scoundrels.

Not only in politics but also on many college campuses, claims of victimhood are like coupons redeemable for numerous petty benefits. Failing work may receive a passing grade, or organized disruption and intimidation may be forgiven and rewarded, or a substandard professor may receive tenure.

There are many people with their own incentives for promoting racial paranoia. But the unintended consequences for blacks and other minorities often far outweigh whatever benefits particular individuals may get out of it.

If we save people like Marion Barry and lose people like the young man at Marquette, we will have made a very bad deal. Attitudes and beliefs which benefit a handful of hustlers do not necessarily benefit a whole race of people—and can in fact be very harmful to that race.

Racial paranoia pictures white people as both all-wicked and all-powerful. If both these beliefs were true, then the whole history of blacks in this country would have been impossible. Blacks were not brought here to become educated or even to play basketball, much less to write books, own property, or sit in Congress. But all this—and more—happened. An earlier generation of black college students understood that they were going to encounter obstacles, but there was no pervasive paranoia that these obstacles were going to stop them.

One of the black professors who taught me during my freshman year at Howard University in Washington was the late and great Sterling Brown. His writings were a bitter and eloquent indictment of racism. But just before I went off to Harvard, he said to me:

"Don't come back here and tell me you didn't make it 'cause white folks were mean."

That was the best advice I could have gotten. It is too bad the young man at Marquette did not get that kind of advice, instead of being fed the paranoid party line.

Are there no more injustices to be concerned about? No more racist attitudes? It would be nonsense to believe that we have reached such a Utopia.

It is bigger nonsense to believe that such a Utopia is a precondition for individual or group advancement. Both in the United States and in other countries around the world, the most successful minority groups have been those who have concentrated their energies on developing their own economic skills—not worrying about the sins of other people.

Often these successful minorities have overtaken the majority in the competition of the marketplace, despite lingering evidences of discrimination.

Attempting the moral regeneration of other people is almost as futile as letting yourself be dominated by racial paranoia or becoming preoccupied by the petty perks of victimhood. Those are blind alleys.

---------------------------------- ◆ ----------------------------------

THE NEW RACIAL ETIQUETTE

THE LATE BAYARD RUSTIN, lifelong black civil rights advocate, gave a talk some years back at a banquet in honor of Norman Thomas. Bayard Rustin recalled how, as a young man, he often took his latest bright ideas to the older man for his comments. More than once, Norman Thomas' response was: "Aw, Rustin, that's a lot of crap!"

"He was the first white man to treat me as an equal," Rustin said at the banquet.

Equality, like everything else, has its down side. But, if it's real equality, you take the bitter with the sweet. Too often today, there is a phoney new racial etiquette in place of equality.

In a thoughtful essay not long ago, author Charles Murray pointed out how the new racial etiquette works to the disadvantage of young black attorneys starting their careers in big law firms. While a young white attorney who makes the kind of stupid mistake that inexperience can lead to may be mercilessly criticized for it, the young black attorney may be handled with kid gloves, for fear of the dreaded suspicion of "racism."

A few years of this kind of difference in treatment can slow the black attorney's development, while the white attorney is learning from the school of hard knocks. Similar things happen in other areas, where a promising and talented young black may never develop his talents fully and fulfill his promise because he is prematurely applauded and seldom hears a critical word.

Man is a highly imperfect creature, no matter what color wrapping he comes in. What often saves us from the worst consequences of our own errors is that each of us is quick to point out the mistakes of others, however blind we are to our own. Exempting anyone from criticism is a disservice, not a favor. But the current racial climate makes equality of criticism hard to achieve.

Back in 1970, I was being considered for an appointment to the economics department at U.C.L.A. As part of the usual practice in such cases, I was invited out to give a talk on some of my current research and to have a discussion about it with members of the department. It so happens that U.C.L.A. has quite a few economists trained at the University of Chicago (as I was) and arguments among Chicago economists can get pretty hot and heavy.

A black woman sitting in the audience during our arguments was appalled as she saw all these white economists tearing into this black economist. She later phoned one of the senior members of the department to complain.

"If you don't want to hire Sowell," she said, "that's your business. But all these people didn't have to attack him like that. I have never seen such hostility!"

"What are you talking about?" he shot back. "These guys love Tom. Of course we are going to hire him."

The bottom line is that I was in fact hired and given tenure at the same time, which was unusual. I never had a better set of colleagues. My writings were improved by their criticisms before the manuscripts were sent off to be published. Many of the young blacks coming along today will never have the benefit of such candid criticisms. Their exemption from criticism often begins while they are still students.

One of the saddest examples occurred recently at Vassar College. According to *The Vassar Spectator*, a student publication, a black student made obscene anti-Semitic statements to a Jewish student at a public gathering. The Vassar Students Association, which supplied the money for the publication, told the editors of *The Vassar Spectator* not to print the story—and cut off their money when they printed it anyway.

The student accused of making anti-Semitic remarks declined to comment. What is shocking is that others leaped to his defense. Although the president of the Vassar Students Association says that the accused student admitted making obscene anti-Semitic statements, these statements were "taken out of context" by *The Vassar Spectator* and this represented "irresponsible journalism," according to her. Another student suggested that the quotes may not have been "100 percent accurate"—and besides, the abusive remarks were made "in the heat of an argument."

The "responsible" college "leadership" has met this whole episode with ringing silence. "It is really a student matter among students," a college spokesman said.

Many young people say and do many things that they never should have. Criticism is one of the things that can help turn them around. The late Supreme Court Justice Hugo Black was a member of the Ku Klux Klan in his youth but, in later years as a member of the high court, he was a consistently strong supporter of the civil rights of blacks.

The young man at Vassar deserves at least a chance to change by being criticized. Instead, the college administration runs for cover and the student organization directs its attack against those who published the story.

Unfortunately, this kind of reaction is all too common on too many campuses across the country. This atmosphere of double standards and doubletalk contributes to the racial backlash that is making many campuses more polarized than they were a generation ago. Ultimately, no one is better off in such an ugly climate.

◆

AN EXCEPTIONAL NEED

THERE ARE EXCEPTIONS TO ALMOST ANY RULE. One of the rules we need to follow in many areas is to stop massive government spending programs and to stop centralizing control in Washington. However, there is one problem that merits an exception, even to this rule.

Many existing college scholarship and loan programs finance minority students who might otherwise be unable to attend, for lack of money. Unfortunately, such programs often finance these students at institutions where many—or most—are almost certain to fail. More than 7 out 10 black students fail to graduate at Berkeley and San Jose State University, for example.

The crux of the problem is that financial aid packages are typically put together by the colleges themselves and are used to produce good public relations for the colleges, which can point to an impressive body count of minority students—even if most of these bodies will never be seen on a graduation platform receiving a degree.

This would be bad enough if the colleges were using their own money to rent minority students as window dressing. But most financial aid money for students does not come from the colleges and universities themselves. Out of $26 billion in financial aid awarded during the academic year 1988–89, nearly $20 billion came either from the federal government or through federally supported programs such as subsidized loans.

Why should the taxpayers' money be used to finance failure, for the greater glory of academic image? What is especially galling is that so many of the minority students who fail are perfectly capable of succeeding at some other college or university. But double standards of admissions lead to widespread mismatching, when body count policies over-ride common sense and common decency.

With the federal government already underwriting a large part of student financial aid, it should take control of that financial aid and use it to finance needy students directly and fully. It has already been vesting benefits in students themselves, for decades, with educational benefits for veterans under the G. I. Bill. The advantages of doing so, for needy students, are many and include social as well as educational benefits.

For minority students, such a policy would mean that they could receive scholarships and loans without having to gamble on going to colleges where their chances of survival are slim. For low-income students who are not members of minority groups, it would mean that they would receive aid based on need, rather than race. One of the recurring sources of intergroup bitterness—in other countries as well as in the United States—is that students from affluent families are receiving financial aid because of the group they belong to, while needy students from other groups are denied the aid they need to pursue their education.

There is no reason in the world why physicians and executives should not pay for their own children's education, regardless of what race they belong to.

In order to provide full support for needy students, the federal government would have to have a substantial increase in scholarship money in many cases, if government grants are to be large enough to replace the colleges' own financial aid packages. But expansion of federal student aid would cost nothing like the vast sums that the government is already pouring into academic institutions for other purposes.

Vast federal research grants—running into billions of dollars—are one source that could be tapped for money for increased spending on financial aid to needy students. Serious research in such fields as medical science or engineering need not be reduced. But there are all sorts of federally financed boondoggles in the so-called "social sciences" which accomplish nothing but to allow professors to get their names in print and avoid having to go into classrooms to teach.

Minority students and other low-income students can receive better opportunities to go to college—and to graduate—without all the needless failures or the polarization and strife that grow out of double standards of admission and financial aid. If it takes a federal program to do that, even conservatives should accept it. The alternative of letting our campuses continue to be breeding grounds for racial strife (that must ultimately spill over into the larger society) is so much worse.

--- ◆ ---

PART VIII
RANDOM THOUGHTS

---------------------- ◆ ----------------------

RANDOM THOUGHTS

SOME RANDOM THOUGHTS ON THE PASSING SCENE:

Ideology is fairy tales for adults.

Thanks to fax machines, we can now get junk mail faster.

Sometimes reformed sinners are such a pain that you wish they had kept on sinning.

The kind of people we need in Washington won't go to Washington.

Envy plus rhetoric equals "social justice."

There is no bigger waste of time than doing 90 percent of what is necessary.

Is this an age of conspiracy theories or what? A popular bumper sticker says: "Humpty-Dumpty was pushed."

Eunuchs are the only "safe sex."

There are people who seem to think that the world owes them an awful lot, but who feel no need to explain what they have contributed to the world that led to this great debt.

Someone said that Congress would take 30 days to make instant coffee.

The older I get, and the more I see of human beings, the more I understand why some people love their dogs so much.

The national debt is the ghost of Christmas Past.

People will forgive you for being wrong, but they will never forgive you for being right—especially if events prove you right while proving them wrong.

Somewhere in this big world, there must be a naive Italian, but I have never met him.

Modern "liberated" women and men have marriages that try to operate democratically. Old-fashioned marriages are more like a constitutional monarchy: The king's pre-eminence is unchallenged, but the prime minister makes the decisions.

No matter how disastrously some policy has turned out, anyone who criticizes it can expect to hear: "But what would you replace it with?" When you put out a fire, what do you replace it with?

We all have our dreams of glory. My dream of glory is to be head of a fire department. Whenever a doctor phoned in to say that his house was on fire, I would tell him to take two aspirin and call me in the morning.

Many bad policies are simply good policies carried too far.

Subtlety counts. If Mona Lisa had broken into a big toothy grin, she would have been forgotten long ago.

One of the lamest excuses for doing something wrong is: "I was just doing my job." A hit man is just doing his job. A prostitute is just doing her job.

With some people, if you give them an inch, they will convert it to centimeters.

It is amazing how much panic one honest man can spread among a multitude of hypocrites.

People who have time on their hands will inevitably waste the time of people who have work to do.

Anyone who feels "entitled" should check the back of his birth certificate. There are no money-back guarantees there, nor even a limited warranty.

One of the greatest gifts in life is the sense to know what problems don't have to be solved and what hassles you don't have to get involved in.

Nobody is equal to anybody. Even the same man is not equal to himself on different days.

If you are not prepared to use force to defend civilization, then be prepared to accept barbarism.

Watching young people letting their opportunities slip away is like watching someone flushing gold down the toilet.

Most sound bites aren't very sound.

The curse of the intelligentsia is their ability to rationalize and re-define. Ordinary people, lacking that gift, are forced to face reality.

People who give money to street beggars out of a sense of guilt ought to feel guilty instead about making an instalment payment on the destruction of American society.

The average intelligence of a committee is always lower than the intelligence of its average member. Committees will often do things more stupid than any member of the committee would have done alone.

"Exact change" fanatics will hold up the longest line for the longest time, while they try to put together exactly $11.88, instead of paying twelve dollars and taking 12 cents change. Sometimes the search for coins to add up to 88 cents will require an exploration of the pockets and handbags of the whole family. The triumphant look of joy when the 88 cents is finally assembled is seldom shared by those waiting in line behind them.

Whenever people refer to me as someone "who happens to be black," I wonder if they realize that both my parents were black. If I had turned out to be Scandinavian or Chinese, people would have wondered what the hell was going on.

If you doubt that women are more complicated than men, try raising a daughter. Raising a son may be hard work, but raising a daughter truly builds character.

What is history but the story of how politicians have squandered the blood and treasure of the human race?

The biggest disappointment is disappointment with yourself.

How can anyone believe that any Congressman can possibly be well informed about all the things that Congress has to vote on?

It is hard for me to sympathize with young people who are trying to "find themselves." When I was their age, I was trying to find the rent.

There are only two kinds of food—Southern fried chicken and everything else.

Back in my old neighborhood, there was a special contempt for the kind of guy who was always trying to get two other guys to fight each other. Today, it is considered a great contribution to society to incite consumers against producers, tenants against landlords, women against men, and the races against each other.

So many children come back home after they have grown up and left that there is now a name for them: "Boomerangs."

Are you paranoid? When you see football players gathered in a huddle, do you think they are gossiping about you?

All human beings are so fallible and flawed that to exempt any category of people from criticism is not a blessing but a curse. The intelligentsia have inflicted that curse on blacks.

According to David Brinkley, a manufacturer of political campaign buttons insists on cash when he sells to politicians, because he has learned from experience that they are deadbeats.

Is there anything more mindless than the endless repetition of the word "change"? Does it make any sense for grown men and women to be either for or against "change" in the abstract? The word covers everything from Hitler to the Second Coming.

A politician once said privately: "I don't mind being a puppet. Just don't let the strings show."

To me, the fact that I have never murdered an editor is proof that the death penalty deters.